Unforced Errors is an appropriate title for this book, which artfully chronicles mistakes made by political leaders throughout history. It's more than an interesting read. It is valuable as well.

– Evan Bayh, former U.S. Senator and Indiana Governor

When we're honest about them, our mistakes teach us more than our successes. Nations are no different, and if our future leaders study Bob Blaemire's invaluable book, they'll be far wiser and we'll all be better governed.

– Mitch Daniels, former Indiana Governor and former president of Purdue University

Why have some of the smartest and shrewdest American politicians made needless blunders that damaged themselves and their country? In *Unforced Errors*, Bob Blaemire chronicles the haste, hubris, stubbornness, and insecurity that lay behind the bad decisions that presidents and presidential candidates came to regret but could not retract.

– Donald A. Ritchie, U.S. Senate Historian Emeritus, Author of *The Columnist*

The market is glutted with books about presidential triumphs—brilliant speeches, successful negotiations with Congress, far-sighted foreign policy decisions. What we need and what Bob Blaemire happily provides—is a reminder of how human our presidents have been. They have good days and bad days, like all of us, and it should come as no surprise that they make mistakes. *Unforced Errors* takes us into the fascinating territory of the missteps, and their consequences, for the nation at large as well as the presidents and other political leaders who committed them.

– Ted Widmer, Macaulay Honors College (City University of New York), Author of *Lincoln on the Verge*

One of the most perplexing questions in American history is why smart, strategic, and successful leaders sometimes support policies and take actions that undermine cherished long-term goals and even sabotage their careers. Bob Blaemire displays and deploys his substantial political experience and considerable wisdom to examine more than a dozen intriguing case studies of political and governmental folly. Exploring why—and how—successful political leaders commit debilitating 'unforced errors' is sobering and instructive. Blaemire provides us with a valuable lens to analyze American politics and to organize our own professional challenges.

– John T. Shaw, Director of the Paul Simon Public Policy Institute, Author of ***The Education of a Statesman: How Global Leaders Can Repair a Fractured World*** and ***JFK In the Senate: Pathway to the Presidency***

Robert Blaemire has been a participant in politics all of his adult life. Born and raised in Indiana, his career began at the age of 18 upon entering George Washington University. His employment with Senator Birch Bayh (D-IN) began in 1967 and concluded with Bayh's election defeat in 1980. Those 13 years saw Bob rise in the Senate Office with campaign experience that began by traveling with the candidate throughout the 1974 re-election campaign and ended as Political Director of the 1980 campaign.

Bob completed his B.A. in Political Science and his M.A. in Legislative Affairs at George Washington University.

After the 1980 defeat, he founded The Committee for American Principles, seeking to combat the growing role and influence of the New Right in political campaigns.

He began providing political computer services in 1982 before it was a business in politics as it is now. He owned his own firm for 17 years and left the business only to write a biography of Senator Bayh, which was published in 2019.

Bob lives in Chevy Chase, Maryland and has two sons, two daughters-in-law, and three grandchildren.

For Cooper, Faye, and Teddy—may their futures be filled with good decisions.

Robert Blaemire

UNFORCED ERRORS:
15 BAD DECISIONS THAT
CHANGED AMERICAN HISTORY

AUSTIN MACAULEY PUBLISHERS®

LONDON * CAMBRIDGE * NEW YORK * SHARJAH

Ordering Information
Quantity sales: Special discounts are available on quantity purchases by corporations, associations, and others. For details, contact the publisher at the address below.

Publisher's Cataloging-in-Publication data
Blaemire, Robert
Unforced Errors: 15 Bad Decisions That Changed American History

ISBN 9798895434185 (Paperback)
ISBN 9798895434192 (Hardback)
ISBN 9798895434215 (ePub e-book)
ISBN 9798895434208 (Audiobook)

Library of Congress Control Number: 2025908348

www.austinmacauleyusa.com

First Published 2025
Austin Macauley Publishers LLC
40 Wall Street, 33rd Floor, Suite 3302
New York, NY 10005
USA

mail-usa@austinmacauley.com
+1 (646) 5125767

It is customary for authors to thank their families for their love and support and this appreciation is no different. My wonderful sons, Nick and Dan, my terrific daughters-in-law, Ana and Carly, and those glorious three grandchildren, Cooper, Faye, and Teddy, make life worth living. I hope that this project will make them proud.

I also want to thank the entire extended Birch Bayh family, those people I worked with for so long while we were all so young and who's friendship and support mean so much to me. My friend Bob Donin first suggested the title for this book and my friend Ted Widmer even tweaked it further. For them, I am also thankful.

And for my special friend and significant other, Kathleen McGuinness, her unwavering support and encouragement as I worked on this book has made it possible. Her patience when I misbehave is greatly appreciated. I'm eternally thankful for the love she has brought into my life.

Table of Contents

Preface   13

John Adams – The Alien and Sedition Act   20

John Quincy Adams – The Corrupt Bargain   30

Thomas Platt – Bury Theodore Roosevelt in the Vice Presidency   41

Theodore Roosevelt – Two Bad Decisions: Term Limits and 1912   49

Woodrow Wilson – The League of Nations   65

FDR – The Internment of Japanese Americans   78

Richard M. Nixon Versus John F. Kennedy – To Debate or
Not to Debate   92

Lyndon Johnson – Quagmire   102

Richard Nixon – Burn the Tapes   116

George H.W. Bush – Read My Lips   133

Al Gore – Keep Away   144

George W. Bush – WMD   155

John Kerry – Swift Boat   166

John McCain – Soccer Mom   175

Honorable Mentions   184

Unforced Errors: 15 Bad Decisions That Changed American
History A Bibliography   193

References   199

Preface

Americans often use terms such as 'To err is human. Or nobody's perfect. Or we all make mistakes'. Of course, this is true, as it is for all of America's leaders through the years.

When Americans think about John F. Kennedy, they are reminded of his presidency, his assassination, the New Frontier, or maybe even the book he wrote for which he won the Pulitzer Prize, 'Profiles in Courage'. The book chronicles decisions by U.S. senators that were acts of courage, brave decisions that made future Americans remember them. But not all decisions made by public officials are like that.

This book is about decisions made in politics or public policy that may be considered unwise; bad decisions that had unintended negative consequences for the decision-maker. This will not include personal decisions like deciding who to marry or whether to get divorced, but rather look at those political and policy decisions that can be considered, at the very least, unwise.

Similarly, a decision like John F. Kennedy's to visit Dallas in November 1963 led to his death but doesn't really qualify as a decision of real political or policy calculation. Lincoln going to Ford's theater would be in that same category. Or, despite how much Warren Harding's cronies tarnished his presidency, decisions leading up to their corruption don't fall into this category.

Also, we have to ignore Clinton's choice to spend private time with Monica Lewinsky. We're talking about political calculations made by political figures, often at the pinnacle of their own success.

Human beings are fallible so there is nothing surprising when a president or a presidential candidate makes a mistake. There have been notable ones, to be sure, several that may have meant the difference between winning and losing. Candidates running for the Democratic presidential nomination in 1988 included Delaware Senator Joseph Biden, who would later serve eight years as vice president and was elected president in 2020.

But Biden's 1988 campaign came to an end after it was revealed that he had plagiarized from a speech given by a member of the British Parliament Neil Kinnock.

Four years later, there was a debate between President George H.W. Bush, businessman Ross Perot, and Arkansas Governor Bill Clinton when Bush looked at his watch as if he was bored or anxious to leave. Clinton won that election, and his Vice President Al Gore was the Democratic nominee in 2000. Gore debated Texas Governor George W. Bush and his audible sighing during one of the debates with Bush did nothing to help his candidacy.

Only four years later and after the Iowa caucus, Democratic Governor Howard Dean virtually submarined his own candidacy with an insane-sounding scream in front of his supporters and TV cameras. And, in this age when anyone can be photographed or captured on video by ubiquitous cell phones, Republican nominee Mitt Romney's campaign in 2012 would have been considerably better off without his 47% comment at a private fundraising event.

He said that 47% of Americans would vote for Obama, those "who are dependent upon government, who believe they are victims, who believe the government has a responsibility to care for them…who believe they are entitled to healthcare, to food, to housing, to you-name-it."

The 47% remarks hurt Romney a great deal and seemed to underscore a suspicion many Americans had that he didn't care about those who are among the neediest in the country, who might need government assistance of some kind. He had been portrayed by President Obama's campaign as an insensitive rich guy and these remarks played right into their hands.

But Romney's remarks, the debate reactions of Bush and Gore, Dean's screams, or Biden's plagiarism don't fall into the category of strategic, carefully considered decisions. Romney misspoke and a book about misspeaking could require many volumes. The other moments were those that each of the candidates would have loved to have back but none may be categorized as carefully considered parts of a calculated strategy.

Few presidential candidates actively campaigned for the office before the mid-19th century and were not actively involved in campaign decisions.

Therefore, far more of these bad decisions are highlighted afterward, when candidates lead their campaign activities and decision-making.

But there are a number of times that presidents and presidential candidates took action after careful consideration that has tarnished their legacy and lived in history as major mistakes. Mistakes from early American history include those by both Adams presidents, John Adams and his son John Quincy.

Not long after the John Quincy Adams presidency came the missteps of William Henry Harrison, followed in the 19th century's bad decisions by President Abraham Lincoln and his successor, Andrew Johnson. But even with history as a guide, major mistaken strategic decisions were made by a larger number of political figures in the 20th century and have continued into the 21st.

There are surely other bad decisions that could have been included in this book. Hopefully, the conclusions about what should be included will not qualify as bad decisions.

1) John Adams – The Alien and Sedition Act

The second president of the United States and one of the truly great men among our founding fathers, John Adams's presidency was tarnished by a policy decision he made as president, one that has often overshadowed the other substantial contributions he made to American history.

The fact that his reputation will always be tarnished by the Alien and Sedition Act is an illustration of the impact a bad decision can have.

2) John Quincy Adams – The Corrupt Bargain

America's sixth president could probably not be elected today. His personality was dour and, while he was greatly respected for his statesmanship and experience, he was a hard man to like.

Whether it was a result of ambition or not is hard to say but Adams made a decision that will forever sully his reputation. He was seeking the presidency in a campaign against former General Andrew Jackson and agreed to a deal with Henry Clay that secured his victory but laid the groundwork for failures to come.

3) Thomas Platt – Bury Theodore Roosevelt in the Vice Presidency

Platt was the political boss of New York at the end of the 19th century; he maneuvered to have Governor Theodore Roosevelt made vice president on the ticket with President McKinley in order to suffocate his political career. McKinley's assassination thrust Roosevelt into the presidency.

4) Theodore Roosevelt – Two Bad Decisions: Term Limits & 1912

His announcement that he would not run for a second full term turned into a mistake he spent most of the rest of his life trying to undo. He compounded that mistake by seeking the presidency again in 1912. Not only did his candidacy destroy the progressive movement within the Republican Party, turning it into the more conservative, stand-pat party it has been since, but his actions prevented him from being the candidate of the GOP in 1916 when he might well have beaten Wilson.

5) Woodrow Wilson – The League of Nations

Wilson's approach to seeking the League of Nations and the barnstorming tour to promote it led to a stroke that incapacitated him for the rest of his presidency.

6) Franklin D. Roosevelt – The Internment of Japanese Americans

A career marked by major achievement and the fact that he was the only president elected more than twice; his decision to corral Japanese Americans and place them in concentration camps at the outset of World War II will forever tarnish his legacy.

7 and 9) Richard Nixon – Two Bad Decisions: To Debate or Not to Debate & Burn the Tapes

In 1960, deciding to debate John. F. Kennedy as well as his decision to visit all 50 states during the campaign qualify as game-changing errors. Without these decisions, Nixon would have been elected that year.

While trying to navigate the Watergate scandal, Nixon made a number of wrong decisions, especially by not destroying the tapes, which destroyed his presidency.

8) Lyndon Johnson – Quagmire

His decisions to pursue victory in Vietnam, based on inaccurate assumptions, destroyed his legacy and cost thousands of lives.

10) George H. W. Bush – Read My Lips

In the 1988 Republican Convention, nominee George H.W. Bush famously pledged, "Read my lips…No New Taxes," a statement that would come to haunt his presidency.

11) Al Gore – Keep Away

As the Democratic nominee for president in 2000, Vice President Albert Gore, Jr. was personally offended by President Bill Clinton's behavior that led to the Lewinski scandal. Despite the fact that Clinton was enormously popular in 2000, Gore decided to avoid appearing with Clinton and basically stayed away from him. Given the closeness of the election result, this decision can be credited with causing Gore's loss.

12) George W. Bush – WMD

The justification for going to war with Iraq was to prevent Saddam Hussein from using weapons of mass destruction. It turned out they didn't exist and yet the war was fought anyway. The United States' reputation suffered, as did Bush's, and many people died as a result of the faulty and misleading intelligence that provided the justification for war.

13) John Kerry – Swift Boat

As the 2004 Democratic nominee for president, John Kerry's reputation was largely based on his Vietnam experience, both as a heroic soldier and as the leader of Vietnam Veterans Against the War. Ads opposing his candidacy made his Vietnam experience appear fraudulent. He made a decision not to respond to those ads and the result was a wholesale undermining of his campaign.

14) John McCain – Soccer Mom

In 2008, Republican presidential candidate Senator John McCain chose Sarah Palin as his running mate. To many Americans, the level of her unreadiness to be a national leader disqualified McCain from the presidency.

John Adams – Gilbert Stuart painting entitled John Adams @ Board of Trustees –
Courtesy National Gallery of Art, Washington, DC

John Adams – The Alien and Sedition Act

The second president of the United States and one of the truly great men among our founding fathers, John Adams's legacy was tarnished by a policy decision he made as president, one that has often overshadowed the other substantial contributions he made to American history.

From an early age, Adams demonstrated his fealty to democratic ideals and stood up for those ideals in a number of ways. One was the incident of the Boston Massacre in 1770. British soldiers fired on an unruly crowd of Boston patriots, killing five. As they faced a trial for this offense, their defense attorney was none other than John Adams.

He faced significant public scorn for his involvement on behalf of the soldiers but felt strongly about the principle that all persons had a right to legal counsel. It was an act of bravery that was consistent with his later actions to be true to republicanism and democratic ideals.

As a co-author of the Declaration of Independence, he served in the Continental Congress and, later, as United States envoy to France, minister to the Netherlands, and minister to the Court of St. James before becoming the nation's first vice president. He was the author of the Massachusetts Constitution, the world's oldest such document.

When George Washington stepped down as the nation's first president after two terms, Adams was elected to that post, the first contested election for the presidency. He was challenged by his old friend and colleague, Thomas Jefferson.

The world had changed for Adams since the days when he served with Jefferson in Philadelphia during the Continental Congress and in Paris as an envoy. They were the closest of friends but Jefferson's rivalry with Alexander Hamilton during the Washington presidency caused the closest of friends to take sides during the formation of the country's first political parties.

Jefferson served as Washington's secretary of state and Hamilton as treasury secretary, but their constant infighting resulted in the formation of the Federalist Party and the Democratic-Republicans.

While Adams considered himself a member of neither party, he sided with positions taken by Hamilton far more often than with Jefferson. Their differences in policy became personal and what was once a close friendship became one of bitter political rivalry, made more acute when they faced off against each other in the election of 1796.

A flaw in the constitution became apparent with that election. The original operation of the Electoral College was to award the presidency to the person with the majority of electoral votes and the vice presidency to the person coming in second. Placing the man in second place, Jefferson, Adams's rival as his vice president was problematic, to say the least. Only a constitutional amendment could change that.

The first 10 amendments, the Bill of Rights, were passed in 1791, soon after the constitution was ratified, and their guarantees of individual freedom were assured by the founders in order to achieve ratification of the basic document. Only one amendment had passed since, the 11th amendment, establishing state sovereign immunity, which had nothing to do with the Electoral College.

When Adams became president, he appeared at his inaugural in a simple broadcloth suit. The clothes of his predecessor, George Washington, and his Vice President Thomas Jefferson, were far more elegant and fancy.

He had made sure his wife Abigail removed the Adams family seal that had been painted on his coach, evidence that he wanted to symbolize simple republican values about which he felt so strongly. These serve as more examples of the ways that Adams lived his philosophy and sought to remain consistent throughout his life. [i]

As president, Adams faced a significant number of crises and issues, chief among them was a possible war with France. He entered the presidency without the high regard that the nation had for Washington. His election margin was a mere three electoral votes and Jefferson became vice president. The Jay Treaty, promulgated during Washington's presidency amid controversies with England, was greatly unpopular.

Negotiated with Great Britain, it was perceived by many Americans as too pro-British and anti-French. The political parties were aligned as pro-British, the Federalists, and pro-French, the Republicans. Adams was considered the head of the Federalists while Jefferson, a Francophile, was considered the head of the Republicans.

In the aftermath of the French Revolution, French leaders became aggressive toward the American government, feeling it should be pro-French because of the alliance during the Revolutionary War and the continuing disputes America had with Britain.

Adams also appointed his son, John Quincy, to an ambassadorial post. Given his son's diplomatic experience and the compliments expressed about him by President Washington, the appointment felt appropriate to Adams but not to several members of Congress.

This was one example of the ways Adams might act honorably and sensibly but tone deaf to the way those actions were perceived by others. In many ways, Adams felt he was trying hard to live up to the republican spirit expressed in the constitution yet was buried under criticism by all sides.

Tensions with France continued. There was the infamous *XYZ Affair*, in which French diplomats sought to bribe American diplomats, moving the country dangerously toward war. The animosity generated toward France became known as the Quasi-War. Adams felt that his envoys had been treated with disrespect and many Americans clamored for war.

Napoleon Bonaparte was now ruling France, and his military victories greatly strengthened him. Adams knew that war with France would not be easy and was committed to keeping the country out of war, to navigate the heated feelings at home while trying to ease the passions caused by actions abroad.

The problems of the Electoral College process as prescribed by the constitution were even more apparent in the election of 1800. Adams and Jefferson opposed each other once again, but this time, the top two candidates who received the most votes were Jefferson and his running mate, Aaron Burr. Adams finished third with only 65 votes.

Because there was no majority winner, Jefferson and Burr were tied with 73 votes each, the election went to the House of Representatives, with each state casting a single vote. There were 16 states in the Union at the time. Jefferson prevailed on the 36th ballot and not until mid-February 1801.

By the end of 1803, Congress passed the 12th amendment to the constitution, which was ratified in June 1804. It separated the electoral votes of the presidential and vice-presidential candidates, so a situation like that endured by John Adams as well as by Jefferson would not happen again.

In many respects, Adams's presidency should have been considered a success simply for the fact that he did keep the country out of war. The appreciation of a grateful nation was not to be his because he was defeated for re-election by Thomas Jefferson before the resolution of the conflict with France. History has also shied away from that appreciation, largely because of the Alien and Sedition Act.

Adams considered these to be war measures and were neither requested nor encouraged by him. Congress sent them to his desk, and he signed them, forever making them part of his historical identity.[ii]

The alien section of the act was a reaction to concerns about foreign visitors to American shores who took part in the criticisms of Adams and the government. It made it easier to deport aliens and increased the time required for immigrants to become citizens from 5 to 14 years.

Adams's behavior demonstrated that he must have had mixed feelings about that section because after considering many efforts by his cabinet to deport aliens, he only signed three orders to do so, all of whom were Frenchmen. The four had, ironically, already left the country.[iii]

The sedition section was more problematic as an assault on freedom of speech and the guarantees of the Bill of Rights.

"The law made any '*False, scandalous, and malicious*' writing against the government, Congress, or the President, or any attempt 'to excite against them…the hatred of the good people of the United States, or to stir up sedition', crimes punishable by fine and imprisonment."

David McCullough, in his masterly biography of our second president, added that "it was clearly a violation of the First Amendment to the Constitution guaranteeing freedom of speech."

The law's supporters justified it as a war measure, even though the war had not yet begun and would not begin.[iv]

To be sure, Adams harbored serious concerns about the political partisanship that was growing up around him. He was frustrated by his inability to get so many other political leaders to stand behind him when he felt he most needed them, oftentimes even members of his cabinet. It was not always apparent that the republic could survive the divisions that were growing in the country. He "worried that the new nation would drift toward factionalism followed by separation or civil war."

Adams had been comfortable in a world where the elites governed. The Alien and Sedition Act of 1798 sprung partly from a concern about "surging populism." During the Adams presidency, the number of newspapers published in the United States grew exponentially, from 100 to more than 250. "Adams was appalled by this noisy babel of new American voices." Among these voices, a number were clearly aligned against him and his policies. The laws against seditious libel were seemingly ignored and he sought a way "to lash out against this new political system that was emerging."

John Adams had always been a champion of free speech, and these new laws were contrary to the republican spirit he was a part of as a member of the revolutionary generation. The public reacted badly to these attempts to stifle free speech, making the political environment even more toxic than it had been. The result was even greater opposition to the Federalists in charge.

The acts led to the party in power "cracking down on the opposition press. In the two years after the Sedition Law was enacted, twenty-five journalists were arrested and ten convicted." One newspaper editor was arrested for publishing a handbill that called Adams incompetent. The arrest, for malicious libel, resulted in a fine and jail time. Even Benjamin Bache, a grandson of Benjamin Franklin was indicted.

Actions like these were not confined to newspaper publishers, however. A member of Congress, Vermont's Matthew Lyon, was jailed because he had a letter to the editor printed in a newspaper referring to the "bullying speech of your president and the stupid answer of your senate." He was found guilty of sedition, sentenced to prison for four months, and fined $1,000, "quite a sum in the days when the median price of an American house was $614." Nonetheless, he was re-elected to the House overwhelmingly. Then, the government "imprisoned a Vermont newspaper editor who had sought to raise money to pay Lyon's fine." [v]

While virtually all those charged were anti-Federalists, later known as Republicans, one rare case where a Federalist was charged under the law came when a judge publicly expressed his reservations about the Alien and Sedition laws. He "was arrested and shipped in irons to New York City for a planned trial." [vi]

When Adams was traveling from the capital in Philadelphia to his home in Quincy, Massachusetts, he and his wife Abigail were passing through Newark, New Jersey, and met with a large celebration.

An elderly and drunken Republican, Luther Baldwin, was watching the entourage when someone near him uttered, "There goes the President and they are firing at his ass." Baldwin's reply was heard by others nearby, "I don't care if they fire through his ass!" That remark led him to be arrested for making an *un-American statement*. He and the man who made the first statement were tried before a circuit court presided over by George Washington's nephew, Bushrod Washington. Both were convicted of speaking "seditious words tending to defame the President and the Government of the United States." They were fined, assessed court costs, and jailed until they were able to pay the fines.[vii]

Adams and his wife Abigail often lived far apart from each other, due to Adams's various postings around the world as well as during the Continental Congress. While serving the early part of his presidency in Philadelphia, the Adams couple were able to live together. They were a loving couple who were very much allies in politics as well. John sought Abigail's views on political matters far more than most presidents in American history.

Because of the attacks on President Adams by Benjamin Bache's newspaper *Aurora*, Abigail wrote, "I wish the laws of our country were competent to punish the stirrer up of sedition, the writer and printer of base and unfounded calumny… This would contribute as much to the peace and harmony of our country as any measure." She felt *Aurora*'s attacks against the government to be undermining the very essence of republicanism.

"It insults the majesty of the sovereign people… Nothing will have an effect until Congress passes a sedition bill."[viii]

"Even George Washington," wrote McCullough, "privately expressed the view that some publications were long overdue punishment for their lies and unprovoked attacks on the leaders of the nation."[ix]

Vice President Jefferson, conversely, drafted the Kentucky Resolutions in response to this law, which passed shortly after the election in which he defeated Adams. They expressed the right of a state to "nullify federal actions it deemed unconstitutional" and seemingly introduced the possibility of secession.[x] Had Jefferson lived another three decades, he would likely have come to regret that action, as southern states seeking to secede led to civil war.

He felt the Federalists "had ground the Bill of Rights under their heel and were certain to keep 'warring against' the 'real principles' on which the new nation stood."[xi]

John Marshall, soon to be chief justice of the Supreme Court, opposed the acts and said that if he had been in Congress, he would have voted against them. His promotion to the Court would be an Adams appointment. James Madison, whom history has labeled as the Father of the Constitution, considered the Act unconstitutional, something most Americans today would agree with.

Even Alexander Hamilton, an opponent of Jefferson and of France, was concerned about the excesses represented by the law. "'Let us not be cruel or violent', he pleaded with party members, warning that, 'there are limits which must not be passed. Let us not establish a tyranny'. Hamilton feared a backlash."[xii]

Those opposed to the Alien and Sedition Act, like Madison and Jefferson, found themselves in a uniquely difficult situation. The Supreme Court had not yet enunciated the principle that it had a right to rule on the constitutionality of Congressional actions. Jefferson and Madison felt the Act to be in direct violation of the first amendment, which said Congress shall make no law abridging the freedom of speech. This law clearly abridged free speech but no institution in government as yet assumed a role in ruling on a law's constitutionality. They looked also to the 10th amendment, which reserved powers not expressly given to Congress to be reserved to the states.

"The powers not delegated to the United States by the Constitution, nor prohibited by it to the States, are reserved to the States respectively, or to the people."

The Alien and Sedition Act did not contain powers expressly delegated to Congress. The inability to effectively nullify the Act led to public frustration and even greater opposition to John Adams.

When Adams took part in the writing of the Declaration of Independence, he did so in participation with Thomas Jefferson and Benjamin Franklin. The relationships among these three men were rich and not without tension and conflict.

Franklin, in a letter he wrote in 1783, said this about John Adams:

"He means well for his country, is always an honest man, often a wise one, but sometimes and in some things, absolutely out of his senses."[xiii]

In many respects, the government was flailing about without George Washington as a stabilizing symbol. The instability Adams saw, led him to support these measures.

The fact that his reputation will always be tarnished by the Alien and Sedition Act is an illustration of the impact a bad decision can have. Historian John Ferling wrote a book about the election of 1800 and described Adams's signing of the Alien and Sedition Act as "the greatest blot on his presidency."[xiv]

Adams could admit that he was often unpopular and understood the reasons why, those aspects of his personality that pushed others away. He had to have resented the popularity of Jefferson while saddled with him throughout his presidency. He also demonstrated a thin skin that had to be a contributing factor in signing legislation that punished his critics and made it illegal for anyone to publicly insult him.

It was also more than a little hypocritical in that Adams freely criticized other leaders in ways that he helped make illegal. He repeatedly wrote to friends that Alexander Hamilton was a "bastard brat of a Scotch ped[d]ler." He also directed his criticism at George Washington, calling him a "muttonhead" and "too illiterate, unlearned, unread, for his station and reputation." [xv]

Yet, the more one studies Adams the more it seems he would have eventually regretted the decision to support the Alien and Sedition law. He had grown frustrated by his contemporaries and the fact that his contributions to the founding of the nation were largely unappreciated.

For much of American history, Adams was a background figure, largely ignored. The U.S. capitol city, Washington, DC, is adorned with monuments to Washington and Jefferson but none to Adams. George Washington has always been considered the Father of the Country and Thomas Jefferson is revered for his authorship of the Declaration of Independence.

Adams himself had encouraged Jefferson to take the lead role in writing the Declaration, both because he saw Jefferson as a better writer and also because he knew, he, Adams, was considered by many in the Continental Congress to be obnoxious. Adams, from Massachusetts, also felt that a Virginian was needed for the task, which Jefferson was.

As slave owners, Washington's and Jefferson's reputations may be more tarnished now than they were in the first two centuries of the country's life. Jefferson's sexual relationship with his slave diminished him in the eyes of many Americans. Yet the honorable, puritan life of John Adams remains largely unappreciated.

He knew that he played a significant and large role in the founding of the United States. David McCullough's biography of Adams brought on a resurgence of interest in him and greater appreciation among the general public than there had been. As historian Joseph Ellis wrote when discussing the celebrations typical of July 4, "The whole country, after all, was celebrating an event that he, more than anyone else, had helped bring about."[xvi]

Was Adams's legacy diminished because he was defeated for re-election? Or was it damaged by his association with the Alien and Sedition Act? It's impossible to know for sure but his decision to support the law was inconsistent with much of what he stood for in his public life. For that reason alone, it must be considered to be a bad decision.

John Quincy Adams – daguerreotype taken in March 1843 by Phillip Haas –
Courtesy National Portrait Gallery, Washington, DC

John Quincy Adams –
The Corrupt Bargain

By the year 1820, American politics had evolved in a manner that would never be seen again. James Monroe, the country's fifth president, would be re-elected without opposition, a time that has been called The Era of Good Feelings.

The demise of the Federalist Party, identified with the nation's second president, John Adams, as well as several other leaders like Congressman Daniel Webster, was nearly complete. Monroe was re-elected by a near unanimous vote in the Electoral College with only a single vote cast for another person, one who was not a candidate.

That person was John Quincy Adams, the son of former President John Adams, with an incredibly distinguished resume. In the Monroe administration, he served as secretary of state, considered the stepping stone to the presidency.

America's sixth president, John Quincy Adams, could probably not be elected today. His personality was dour and, while he was greatly respected for his statesmanship and experience, he was a hard man to like. Kissing babies would certainly never occur to him but it would be a mistake to assume he was not ambitious.

His ambition may have been the result of his trying to fulfill parental expectations since he was probably the first American ever groomed to be president from the earliest years of his life. He traveled with his father, the country's second president and one of the most prominent of America's founding fathers, to countries abroad when most Americans never left the communities in which they lived.

He experienced the courts of Europe at a tender age and was trained in the skills required of a diplomat.

Born on July 11, 1767, and named after his mother's maternal grandfather, Colonel Quincy, he watched the Battle of Bunker Hill from a hill near his house in Quincy, named for the same great-grandfather. He was only eight years old. His father John was a prominent man in the Massachusetts colony and had high expectations for his firstborn. When 11 years old, he accompanied his father on a diplomatic mission in Europe, spending six weeks on board a ship crossing the Atlantic.

He grew to be 5' 7" tall, athletic, and was an avid swimmer. Fluent in French, Dutch, and German, and proficient in Italian, Latin, and classical Greek, he attained bachelor's and master's degrees from Harvard. He would go on to serve as minister to Great Britain and to the Netherlands, Prussia, and Russia.

At age 30, he married the 22-year-old Louisa Catherine Johnson, who would become the first foreign-born first lady. Adams served as secretary of state for eight consecutive years under President James Monroe and is considered one of the most accomplished secretaries of state of all time.

He was a proponent of manifest destiny until it became clear that the national movement toward expansion also meant the expansion of slavery, to which he was intensely opposed.

Much of what we know about John Quincy Adams and how he thought comes from the diary he kept, beginning at age 12 and maintained until his death in 1848. It reveals that he suffered from depression for much of his life.

His rectitude and seriousness about public service dominated his life from childhood on. But he never seemed to put a priority on interpersonal relationships or a sense of humor. In short, he was a hard man to like but an easy man to admire and respect. He was ambitious but more for his country than for himself and certainly never for personal financial gain. Never, it seemed, did he shed the weight of expectations placed upon him at a very early age.

The two presidents prior to his own presidency, James Madison and James Monroe, had both acceded to the office after serving as secretary of state. They were the fourth and fifth presidents. Thomas Jefferson was the third president and, while he won the office by defeating the second president, John Quincy's father John Adams, Jefferson had also served as secretary of state under George Washington. In other words, serving as secretary of state was the stepping stone to the White House and, in 1824, it was John Quincy Adams's turn.

Historian Samuel Flagg Bemis wrote about Adams: "Only in such a quiet time could a man like John Quincy Adams ever be elected President. He led no party, controlled no political machine, nor did he have the personal magnetism or other qualities necessary to build one. All he had to stand on politically was his distinguished lineage, his character, his large experience with affairs at home and abroad, and his undoubted competence for public office. No man has ever been better fitted, as professional public servant, for the Presidency. No man has had less aptitude or inclination for the organization and command of political cohorts."[xvii]

While Adams had held a significant number of important positions in the American government, they were all by appointment, none by election. His few efforts at popular election had not gone well.

He was defeated in his first contest for Massachusetts state assemblyman and, after being elected U.S. senator by the Massachusetts legislature in 1803, he was later removed because of his stubborn independence. He did not like appealing to voters and was comfortable relying on the judgment of the elites who ran America's politics.[xviii]

What Adams faced in 1824, however, was a popular groundswell in the country that threatened to take away the presidential choice from America's elite, the leaders who seemed destined to make that decision. It was the purpose behind the creation of the Electoral College and a tradition of popular voting had not yet settled in.

As states made the franchise available to white males at least 21 years of age without a land-owning requirement, it made sense that someone who didn't come from among the elites would soon rise to power. Andrew Jackson was that man.

Jackson had been the hero of the Battle of New Orleans at the end of the War of 1812. It had been the most one-sided victory of that war. The British had lost about 2,000 men while Jackson's forces lost less than 100. He had been hailed not only by his soldiers for this great success but by the country at large. By the early 1820s, there was a movement to make him president.

Comparing Jackson to Adams, the contrast couldn't be starker. As proper as Adams was in every respect, Jackson was an avid horseman, hot-tempered, and had killed a man in a duel. Having a man like Jackson become president would have been repulsive to Adams even if it didn't mean that he himself would not be elected.

On CNN's 'Race for the White House' during March-April 2016, there was an examination of the many facets of this competition.

Jackson was considered to be a person who would kill to get his way. He was known to have exceeded his orders in his military past. As personally popular as he was, those in power saw him as a potential dictator who could not be allowed near the reins of power. Nonetheless, Jackson became a candidate, and the battle was on in the election of 1824.

While the country was experiencing an inexorable movement toward popular democracy, the waning powers still belonged to Congressional leaders and political leaders in several states, particularly in state legislatures. Candidates were promoted in various fashions to compete with Adams and Jackson.

There was Secretary of the Treasury William H. Crawford of Georgia, Speaker of the House of Representatives Henry Clay of Kentucky, and Secretary of War John C. Calhoun of South Carolina.

Adams had been an admirer of Jackson, though couldn't abide the possibility that Jackson could be president, but held his greatest contempt for Crawford, who he considered unscrupulous.

In discussing Crawford and the pending campaign with President Monroe, Adams said, "What chance against him will a man have who neither can nor will use such means?" [xix]

Crawford, however, suffered a stroke in September 1823, which negatively affected his ability to seek the high office. As for Clay, Adams respected the speaker and agreed with the Kentuckian's efforts to seek internal improvements in America's infrastructure. Adams considered his fellow cabinet member, John C. Calhoun, to be a friend. That friendship would be strained by the campaign.

Calhoun, moreover, did something that has never taken place in American history. He ran for vice president when it became clear he didn't have the support for the top office. But he ran as the running mate for both Adams and Jackson. He would be elected vice president twice, once each for both Adams and Jackson. Adams had actually preferred Jackson to be his running mate, but Jackson made it clear that he had no interest in the second spot on anyone's ticket.

In that era, however, it was considered unseemly for candidates to openly pursue the office. They did not campaign, except behind the scenes. Adams considered the office of the president to be "a family inheritance" and "an object of pursuit." He may have dearly wanted the presidency but expected it to come to him as it did to Washington, "unsolicited, unconnived for, without commitments or bargains with any man, a prize for which he, the son of President John Adams and Abigail, would not lift a finger or make a nod. 'If my country wants my services, she must ask for them'."[xx]

Adams was encouraged to be more active by friends and said to one, "My business is to serve the public to the best of my abilities in the station assigned to me, and not to intrigue for further advancement. I have never, by the most distant hint to anyone, expressed a wish for any public office, and I shall not now begin to ask for that which of all others ought to be most freely and spontaneously bestowed."[xxi]

America in 1824 was a country made up of 24 states. The Electoral College was comprised of the combined number of members of the House (213) and Senate (48), 261 votes in all. Electors were not chosen by popular vote in all states but for those states that did record their popular votes, the results reflected the Electoral College vote count.

Andrew Jackson earned 99 electoral votes to Adams's 84. Crawford won 41 votes and Clay trailed with 37. Of the popular vote, Jackson won a similar plurality with 153,544 votes to Adams's 108,740. Clay won 47,136 with Crawford coming in fourth at 46,618.

But the constitution requires that a majority vote be obtained, meaning the election was to be determined by the House of Representatives, with each state casting a single vote. A majority of 13 states would determine the winner; 213 men would choose the president.

The number of men deciding the vote of each state was small. There were four states with only a single member in the House and the largest state by population was New York, with 34 members. If the 13 smallest states voted en bloc, only 46 Congressmen would be making the decision.

The election campaign shifted to one directed at these men serving in Congress and for that, Adams held a distinct advantage. When Andrew Jackson arrived in Washington with his wife Rachel, they stayed at a boarding house. Rachel was not sophisticated and detested Washington. Her attitude prevented the Jacksons from mixing socially in a way they otherwise might have.

Adams, on the other hand, with his cultured wife, was able to wine and dine congressmen in his home. Louisa Catherine Adams was entirely comfortable while entertaining these men.

But more importantly, the speaker of the House was Henry Clay of Kentucky, the "most powerful legislator of his time," as described by National Public Radio's Steve Inskeep.

Inskeep, also a Jackson biographer, characterizes him by writing, "Jackson was a passionate man and a killer."[xxii]

Clay was as ambitious as any man in Washington and saw Jackson for the threat he was, particularly to Clay's own hopes for the presidency. He huddled with Adams and the result of their conversations has sullied the reputation of John Quincy Adams ever since.

Clay's assessments of the different candidates made Adams an obvious choice. Having come in fourth in the Electoral College count, he was not eligible to be considered by the House. He had a serious concern about Jackson's militarism and the role that might play in a Jackson presidency as well as the popularity he represented, which could be a barrier to Clay's own presidential hopes.

Clay considered Crawford too unwell to serve, leaving only Adams, whom Clay knew would preserve America's institutions as they were. He would be determined to cut a deal in his personal interest while also supporting the man who would be the best choice as president.

This man of high morality, John Quincy Adams, has forever been described as an unseemly deal maker, one who agreed to what has become known as the *corrupt bargain*. The House of Representatives, with each state having a single vote, voted Adams into the presidency and Speaker Clay became secretary of state, still assumed to be the stepping stone to that high office.

Adams was advised that Clay held sway over the votes in three states Adams had lost, Clay's Kentucky plus Ohio and Missouri. As it turned out, Adams ended up winning all three although he hadn't received a single popular vote in Kentucky, which was split between Jackson and its favorite son Clay.[xxiii]

The election wasn't resolved until February 9, 1825, and Adams was elected with a bare majority of 13 states. The Adams verdict was one determined by politicians, not the people. In fact, he won the vote of three states in the House of which he lost the popular vote.

When an ally of Clay, Kentuckian Robert Letcher, approached Adams about the importance of an Adams victory on the first ballot in the House, Adams knew he was playing with fire. "*Incedo super ignes* [I am treading coals of fire]," was his entry in his diary.[xxiv]

Yet the man who assiduously wrote in his diary throughout his life was strangely silent during the negotiations with Henry Clay, which began shortly after the election but before the deliberations in the House of Representatives. After they met several times, it was clear that Clay assumed that any cabinet office he might want would be his. As speaker of the House, he would have greater sway over his colleagues than anyone else.

One of Adams's advisors was George Sullivan of New Hampshire, also a close friend of John C. Calhoun. Sullivan warned the president-elect that Calhoun sought to be the real power in the administration, and that appointing Henry Clay to be secretary of state would motivate Calhoun to organize an opposition to Adams.

Calhoun, like a shark smelling blood in the water, understood the Clay appointment to be toxic to the president himself. Should Adams fall after a single term, Jackson would replace him, and Calhoun could then be in line to succeed the Tennessean himself. Adams asked Sullivan whom he had heard that scenario from and Sullivan told him he came straight from the mouth of Calhoun. "I am at least forewarned," thought Adams.

The Era of Good Feelings was definitely over. Jackson viewed the election as stolen, described the Clay appointment as a "corruption and bargain" [xxv] and many wondered what he might do. Shortly after the election was resolved, he described the deliberations in the House of Representatives, where it was to be decided, with some bitterness. "It shows the want of principle in all concerned." Once the House elected Adams, and after Clay quickly accepted his appointment as secretary of state, Jackson called Clay *the Judas of the West* and *his end will be the same.*

Later, he added, "If at this early period of the experiment of our Republic, men are found base and corrupt enough to barter the rights of the people for proffered office, what may we not expect from the spread of this corruption hereafter."[xxvi] It was in his nature to be outraged by insults or injustice and the election defeat created a resolve in him to correct the injustice and overturn the result. He would have four years to accomplish that task. To the surprise of many, he behaved graciously.

Martin Van Buren, a New York politician, allied himself with Jackson to bring down the powerful men who were in charge. He saw the battle as one between the people and the elites. Their partnership represented the early beginnings of the Democratic Party.

Van Buren understood how to use the growing number of newspapers to their advantage and aggressively provided them with stories designed to make Adams unpopular and to promote General Jackson. The plethora of articles turned Jackson into a celebrity, far beyond a typical political figure. His growing fame made him legendary.

At the same time, Adams would not allow his office to be used to build up his own popularity. Having made the deal known as the corrupt bargain, he wouldn't take the steps that were needed to ensure his own re-election. Even though Adams promoted internal improvements by the government, the building of roads, bridges, and dams, and those improvements were very popular, they didn't translate into presidential popularity.

Clay quickly saw what was happening and understood what the bargain had done to his own popularity. As he saw it, if Adams wouldn't work to make himself popular, Clay would work to make Jackson unpopular. He'd go after Jackson's Achilles heel.

As Steve Inskeep said, it was "one of the great smear campaigns of its time."

Clay spread stories about Jackson killing his own soldiers. The general had presided over a number of executions for dereliction of duty or desertion, but those actions were portrayed as inhumane and unnecessary. Jackson's military reputation was his greatest strength. But the issue on which he was the most sensitive involved his wife, Rachel. In fact, reacting to an insult to Rachel, Jackson had once killed a man in a duel.

Rachel had left her husband, Lewis Robards, many years earlier and had married Jackson after hearing that Robards had divorced her. When they learned that the story of the divorce was not accurate, they found themselves in a bigamist marriage.

Clay took the facts of the bigamy to the newspapers and its salacious details caught the imagination of anyone who was not a stalwart Jackson supporter. He added to those articles a constant stream of ridicule about Jackson's inability to spell, citing letters and handwritten documents over a long period of years.

Clay hoped for a violent reaction, something that would reinforce his view that Jackson was unfit to be president. Instead, the Jackson forces floated a rumor that when Adams was minister to Russia, he had procured a woman for the Czar. In effect, they were calling the president a pimp.

However, the anniversary of the Battle of New Orleans had arrived, and it was the occasion for Jackson to make a lengthy, triumphant procession to New Orleans from his home in Nashville. The crowds he attracted were huge and enthusiastic, something very difficult to ignore. The celebration became national, and Jackson found himself at the center.

The intense partisanship of the period resulted in Adams creating a cabinet only of allies, no one who had opposed his election besides Clay. There was a dearth of strong, ambitious men and the cabinet proved unable to become an important ally of President Adams. Disagreements with Secretary Clay began, and Clay threatened to leave the cabinet. Adams pleaded with him to stay, even suggesting that Clay take a long vacation, one that would require the president to remain in Washington during the summer in order to carry out Clay's duties himself. It was not a happy presidency.[xxvii]

As the election of 1828 approached, it was clear that the campaign was a repeat of the one four years earlier. Jackson could hold the corrupt bargain and the president's elitism against Adams while his own wide popularity and celebrity offered the country a clean break from the past. While the campaign can be described as the most vitriolic to date, it culminated in a rousing success for the populist general from Tennessee.

Looking back at the bargain struck between John Quincy Adams and Henry Clay, it clearly resulted in Adams's election to the presidency. But it can be argued that it strengthened the resolve of Andrew Jackson for revenge and a desire to prevail over Adams that might not have been the same had they won without the apparent quid pro quo.

It has also sullied the reputation of Adams, something that should have been anathema to a man like him, driven to serve the public and live up to the high expectations under which he always lived.

It is ironic that the first two presidents to serve only a single term and denied re-election would be the Adams father and son. The bad decisions made by both men contributed greatly to this unhappy, historic distinction.

John Quincy Adams was an honorable man and saw himself that way. And his commitment to public affairs was undeniable. Being party to an event that would tarnish his reputation seems to be unacceptable, but he did just that. A distinguished career begun at a very young age would continue past his presidency.

He would be elected to the House of Representatives, the only former president to do that, and would spend his remaining years as an anti-slavery champion. He badgered Congress about slavery throughout his tenure and even provided a legal defense for the slaves arrested after commandeering the slave ship *Amistad*.

Did he believe that the end justified the means, that entering into the deal with Henry Clay was worth it in order for him to reach the presidency? It is impossible to know but the connection of his name to the corrupt bargain could not have been something he would have approved of.

Could Adams have won the election without cutting that deal? Perhaps not, but we'll never know. Would Clay have swung the election to Adams without the agreement to make him secretary of state, seemingly next in line for the presidency?

Possibly not. But agreeing to the bargain has tarnished the reputations of both men and was likely the key ingredient in Jackson's commitment to prevail four years hence.

Thomas C. Platt from Appleton's Magazine, 1903

Thomas Platt – Bury Theodore Roosevelt in the Vice Presidency

"My country in its wisdom contrived for me the most insignificant office that ever the invention of man contrived or his imagination conceived."[xxviii]

That was a description of the office of the vice president by its first occupant, John Adams. Almost 150 years later, it was also described derisively by Franklin Roosevelt's first vice president, John Nance Garner. Indelicately, with a sanitized version he called the office *not worth a bucket of warm spit*.

By the time of the last presidential election in the 19th century, that of Ohio Governor William McKinley in 1896, 23 men had served as president; McKinley would be the 24th. One president, Grover Cleveland, served two separate terms, meaning the 24th person would be the 25th president.

But only seven men who served as vice president acceded to the presidency. Of that number, two became president after presidential deaths in office and two more by assassination. Only three vice presidents were elected president in their own right and none since Martin Van Buren in 1836. The vice presidency was hardly a stepping stone to the presidency. It was more of a graveyard.

The Gilded Age is a label describing the United States in the last three decades of the 19th century. Adults born before the Gilded Age would remember well what it was like without indoor plumbing and the advantages brought about by electricity.

The era saw the innovations that would forever change the world – automobiles, airplanes, telephones, as well as indoor plumbing and the harnessing of electricity. Life was so different at the end of the century than it had been in the beginning or even the middle, a period dominated by the Civil War.

What had not changed was the smoke-filled backroom, the way political leaders were selected. It was still an era of the bosses, the political giants, often in the shadows, who would determine the persons to fill a given office. And it was also the era of the rise of Theodore Roosevelt.

Theodore Roosevelt, also known as TR, rose in politics like a rocket. By the age of 40, he had been a New York state legislator, president of New York City's board of police commissioners, United States civil service commissioner, assistant secretary of the Navy, and governor of New York.

He was also an author of 18 books, had been a rancher in South Dakota, and a volunteer militia leader, a Rough Rider, in the Spanish-American War. It was in the latter role that his national profile emerged; leading a charge up San Juan Hill in Cuba during that war created a legend around his name. In New York, his reputation was without blemish.

But there were leaders who found the TR style unattractive, possibly even dangerous. After the election to the presidency of Benjamin Harrison in 1888, for whom Roosevelt had campaigned aggressively, TR wanted to be appointed an assistant secretary of state.

After Harrison's inauguration, the new secretary of state, James G. Blaine, appraised Roosevelt's nature when he wrote, "My real trouble in regard to Mr. Roosevelt is that I fear he lacks the repose and patient endurance required in an Assistant Secretary. Mr. Roosevelt is amazingly quick in apprehension. Is there not danger that he might be too quick in execution?"

Roosevelt was offered the post of civil service commissioner instead.[xxix]

The political boss of New York was Thomas Platt. Platt entered politics before Theodore Roosevelt was born. He campaigned for the first nominee of the new Republican party, John C. Fremont, in 1856 and was elected to Congress in 1872. By 1881, he was a United States senator, the same year that Roosevelt was first elected to the New York State Assembly.

James Garfield became president the same year and immediately entered into a power struggle with the boss of New York at that time, Senator Roscoe Conkling. Conkling's trusted assistant during the dispute over patronage, specifically the appointment of collector of customs for the port of New York, was his Senate colleague Thomas Platt.

The conflict reached a tipping point when both senators resigned their positions, expecting to be sent back to the Senate by the New York legislature and would, then, be more powerful than previously. Senators were not voted on by the electorate at the time but by each state legislature.

Surprisingly, the state legislators did not rush to the defense of Conkling and Platt, refusing to vote them back to the U.S. Senate. Some of their opponents followed Platt into an Albany hotel and, upon entering his room, found him having sex with a woman other than his wife.[xxx]

Platt stepped aside from the effort to return to the Senate but behind the scenes was able to quietly take control of the New York Republican organization. His efforts were made easier by the assassination that same year of President Garfield. It took Platt a few years of toiling in the background of Republican Party affairs, but he was firmly in control by 1887. He supported Roosevelt's unsuccessful candidacy for mayor of New York City in 1886.

Platt's views about Theodore Roosevelt began to change after the election of President Benjamin Harrison. Whether it was jealousy that Platt had received no presidential appointment while TR was appointed civil service commissioner or a difference of opinion about the necessity of civil service reform, which Roosevelt favored, or patronage, which Pratt controlled, doesn't matter.

He watched TR with distaste. When Platt's candidate for mayor, William Strong, was elected and appointed TR as police commissioner, those negative feelings intensified. And the feelings were mutual.

Roosevelt "declared that he was 'astounded' at Platt's success 'in identifying himself with the worst men and worst forces in every struggle, so that a decent man must oppose him'."[xxxi]

Platt and Roosevelt were at war, and it became very public. It seemed that everything Roosevelt did became very public. TR made a name for himself as police commissioner but grew weary of the post as the 1896 presidential campaign loomed ahead. He campaigned hard for William McKinley and nurtured a close relationship with McKinley's manager and chairman of the National Republican Party, Mark Hanna.

With McKinley's election, Roosevelt made it clear that he aspired to become assistant secretary of the Navy. With the help of a prominent McKinley donor, lobbying by Senator Henry Cabot Lodge, and the relationship with Mark Hanna, Roosevelt received the appointment.

Prior to getting the nod, however, Thomas Platt was once again elected U.S. senator in New York. U.S. senators from a newly elected president's party are traditionally given the right of approval for presidential appointments of their own constituents. Roosevelt sought a rapprochement with Platt, who decided to allow the Roosevelt appointment to take place, likely because it removed Roosevelt from New York.

From his post in the Navy Department, Roosevelt took actions when the secretary was out of town which should have gotten him fired. His brazen, aggressive behavior made many people love him and many others hate him. He left the department after the outbreak of the Spanish-American War, creating his own battalion of soldiers to fight in Cuba.

These were the Rough Riders, a colorful but able assembly of men from across America. TR was their undisputed leader, and his own colorful behavior attracted the attention of newspaper reporters from everywhere.

The high-pitched voice, the pince-nez spectacles, the specially tailored uniform, and his reputation as a politician and reformer made him great copy. And now, he was fighting for his country and would do it in a manner that garnered him even greater attention. He would lead a successful charge up Cuba's San Juan Hill on horseback that thrilled Americans reading about it at home.

Returning from the war after its successful conclusion, he was possibly as famous as any American. Like it or not, Thomas Platt couldn't ignore this reality. Platt had opposed the war as a senator and was disgusted by Roosevelt's gung-ho behavior. But as a political realist first and foremost, Platt had to put his feelings aside.

A sitting United States senator and a former member of the U.S. House of Representatives, Platt hardly left a mark in Congress but loomed large over the affairs of the New York Republican Party. He controlled the extensive system of patronage that existed at the time, job placements that were made by elected officials. Republican elected officials owed their allegiance to the man who engineered their elections or appointments. Platt bowed to reality, realizing how popular TR was, and decided that he would be an ideal candidate for governor of New York in 1898.

Roosevelt was promoted to be New York governor by reformers and independents throughout the state. Platt knew that Roosevelt could win but needed him to be the Republican nominee, not an independent choice of non-Republicans. They met and TR agreed to run as a Republican. The organization got in line behind him, and he was elected governor in 1898, less than two weeks after turning 40.

Roosevelt was elected in a competitive election that saw him traveling the length and breadth of the state. This was not common at the time, but TR seemed to love the activity. Once in office, he launched a series of reforms that alarmed the political powers in New York, epitomized by Thomas Platt.

From pushing the legislature to enact the eight-hour workday, he also promoted child labor laws, protections for women and children in the workplace, instigated factory inspections in order to improve working conditions, and setting aside land for conservation.

But most alarming of all for Platt and his cohorts was the first-ever enactment of taxes on business. It was business that financed Platt and those like him, corporations that expected their political patrons to protect them from things like taxation.

The American president first elected in 1896 was, as already mentioned, William McKinley of Ohio. McKinley was governor of the state and ran his presidential campaign from his home, what became known as the *front porch campaign*.

Like in New York, there was a boss in charge who loomed largely over Ohio politics, Mark Hanna. Hanna financed McKinley's campaign after having failed to secure the presidential nomination for Ohio Senator John Sherman in the previous election. His efforts at taking his boss' role in Ohio to the nation at large were finally successful when McKinley secured the nomination.

That same year, Hanna was appointed U.S. senator when Sherman became secretary of state. Once McKinley became president, Hanna was America's political master but operated largely behind the scenes.

On November 21, 1899, Vice President Garret A. Hobart died. In less than a year, President McKinley would be seeking re-election, and the bosses were faced with the decision on the vacancy created by Hobart's death. Platt saw an opportunity to fix his Roosevelt problem by elevating him to the vice presidency in 1900. His Senate colleague, Mark Hanna, shared Platt's attitude about the vice presidency. It was traditionally a burial ground for politicians.

McKinley was America's 25th president. Only four times in American history had a vice president acceded to the presidency while serving as vice president. Presidents William Henry Harrison and Zachary Taylor had died in office while Abraham Lincoln and James Garfield were assassinated. No vice president had successfully run for president since Martin Van Buren, so the safety of that vice-presidential graveyard seemed secure.

As Hanna got to know him better, he considered Roosevelt to be a maniac. He would have sympathized with Platt's desire to remove him from the New York governorship, but Hanna was more concerned than Platt about the national danger TR represented.[xxxii]

But Platt's concern centered more on New York than on the national ticket. Still seeing the vice presidency as a political graveyard, it was a logical move for Platt to try and move TR away from the New York governor's office and ensconce him in a political grave.

"I want to get rid of the bastard," he proclaimed.[xxxiii]

Platt was hearing increasing panic from the New York business establishment. In addition to those measures already sought by the gubernatorial reformer, he was rumored to be considering further altruistic reforms. When Platt was given the drafts of Roosevelt's message to the legislature for 1900, his internal alarm bells rang more loudly.

He was promoting more rigorous controls over public utility companies, allowing greater government inspection of the internal workings of corporations, and reforming the state's lumbering laws in order to protect birds. As hard as all of that was for Platt to digest, he was particularly incensed by TR's plan to remove the corrupt Insurance Commissioner Louis Payn.

Platt's allies in the legislature might protect him from legislative reforms but the governor had the power to dismiss Payn at the expiration of Payn's term in January 1900. Payn was an aging bureaucrat who provided cover for corrupt practices by businessmen across the state. Future Secretary of State Elihu Root, once described him as "a stench in the nostrils of the people of the State of New York."[xxxiv]

Platt forged an alliance with Pennsylvania Senator Matthew Quay to maneuver the Republican Convention toward nominating Roosevelt for the second spot on the McKinley ticket.

As the dates of the convention grew closer, Platt was quoted as saying, "Roosevelt might as well stand under Niagara Falls and try to spit water back as to stop his nomination by this convention."[xxxv]

Hanna did not want him on the ticket but was tardy in his realization that Senators Platt and Quay had made great strides in advancing the Roosevelt candidacy. Hanna actually tried to use McKinley's patronage to persuade delegates to switch their allegiance to another candidate. He had been at odds with Roosevelt for years, though they began their relationship on very good terms.

They came to detest each other; Roosevelt felt that Hanna was "one of those over-grasping plutocrats who believed that because business was good for the country, then business ought to run the government." Hanna was opposed to the war with Spain, largely because it "would be bad for the nation's recently revived economy," bristling over the jingoism that so typified TR.[xxxvi]

Platt and Quay understood the grassroots popularity of Governor Roosevelt, the legendary Rough Rider, and used it to their advantage in promoting his possible candidacy.

A frustrated Hanna argued with the president over the telephone from the convention, finally emerging to say, when asked what the matter was, "Matter! Matter! Why, everybody's gone crazy! What is the matter with all of you? Here's this convention going headlong for Roosevelt for Vice President. Don't any of you realize that there's only one life between that madman and the Presidency? Platt and Quay are no better than idiots! What harm can he do as Governor of New York compared to the damage he will do as President if McKinley should die?"[xxxvii]

After the convention, Hanna wrote to McKinley, "Your duty to the country is to live for four years from next March."[xxxviii]

Typically, Roosevelt campaigned aggressively, something virtually unknown at the turn of the century. While McKinley remained in the White House, Roosevelt whistle-stopped over 20,000 miles, giving 600 speeches in 500 towns in 24 states.[xxxix] The McKinley-Roosevelt ticket was elected in a landslide.

Six months after Roosevelt was sworn in as vice president, President McKinley was assassinated. Theodore Roosevelt was president of the United States and the country, as well as its politics, would never be the same.

Possibly, the most dynamic political figure to ever become president, Roosevelt fulfilled his role magnificently. With his outsized personality, intellectual curiosity, and adventurous streak, he would have been a biographer's dream subject even if his tenure in the White House had been unremarkable. But his presidency – highlighted by his domestic program (the

Square Deal), confrontation with corporate titans, environmental activism, and aggressive internationalism – was instead among the most consequential in history.[xl]

Regardless of how one believed in his politics or policies, his giant presence in office was undeniable. The dominant figure in the first decade of the 20th century, Roosevelt changed the way the world looked at the United States as well as the way Americans viewed their own country. From trust-busting to conservation to progressive policies in untold areas of American life, Theodore Roosevelt dominated American life and changed the country forever.

From the standpoint of the goals embraced by Thomas Platt, his decision to push Governor Theodore Roosevelt into the vice presidency was a bad decision indeed.

Theodore Roosevelt – Two Bad Decisions: Term Limits and 1912

Theodore Roosevelt, while not a tall man, was an outsized character in American history, particularly at the dawn of the 20th century. It seems appropriate that he would be cited for not one bad decision, but for two, decisions that seriously affected the nation for a long time to come.

Reading a resume of TR, as he was known, makes the reader feel woefully inadequate. By the time he was 42 years old, he had served in the New York state legislature, served as a civil service commissioner, and been the police commissioner of New York City. He was also assistant secretary of the Navy, elected governor of New York, and then vice president of the United States. And in 1901, he became president of the United States.

In between all of that, he spent time as a cowboy and cattle rancher in the western U.S., a leader of the Rough Riders in the Spanish-American War, read a book a day, and authored 18 books.

One colorful comment made to Roosevelt as he faced his election campaign in 1904 and reached the ripe old age of 46 was made by Elihu Root. Root was a distinguished public servant who would later serve as TR's secretary of state.

In the words of Roosevelt biographer Edmund Morris, Root *developed an almost paternal tenderness* for Roosevelt, sending him a birthday note one year that read, "You have made a very good start in life and your friends have great hopes for you when you grow up."[xli]

Theodore Roosevelt – Courtesy the Library of Congress

Bad Decision #1

First, it's important to know that Roosevelt made many great, substantive decisions in his career, measures that changed America in a number of ways. He challenged child labor laws, and the economic power of the trusts, expanded America's national parks, and was a reformer of the first order. He fought public corruption throughout his varied career.

But it's fair to suggest that much of what he did was also damaged by the two bad decisions discussed here. Those two decisions are also very much linked together, the second one unlikely to happen without the first one having taken place.

Republican Party leaders conspired to make Roosevelt the vice president because of the way his reforms as governor were threatening their status quo. The vice presidency was considered a political graveyard and when President McKinley's vice president died during his first term, Roosevelt was promoted to replace him. Six months after he was sworn in as vice president, President McKinley was assassinated, and TR became president.

Roosevelt burst upon the national scene like no president before him. His activism and dynamism were impressive, and his young family caught the public's attention with affection. He was everywhere all the time it seemed, and the measures being pressed upon the Congress from the White House were breathtaking.

The staid, conservative men who had held the presidency during the lifetimes of most Americans of that era were nothing like this new form of politician holding the office.

Roosevelt loved the presidency, which he described as *the greatest office in the world*.[xlii] He was a man of action and entirely comfortable as the most visibly active man in the nation. But he was also impetuous. In the immediate aftermath of his 1904 election to a full term as president, he announced that he would not be a candidate again in 1908.

His announcement that he would not run for a second full term was highlighted in a 1996 production of Public Television's series, 'The American Experience', a documentary called 'TR', produced by David Grubin. The incident of that announcement was articulated well.

At the end of his first term in office, completing the unfinished presidency of the assassinated William McKinley, Roosevelt ran on his own and was elected. His election was a ringing endorsement of his presidency and of him personally. Winning 33 of the 45 states, he outpolled the popular vote of President McKinley when they ran together four years earlier. At that point, he was almost the exact age his father had been when he died.

It was almost as if he couldn't imagine himself living longer than his father when he called together a group of reporters on that election night and told them, "On the fourth of March next, I shall have served three and a half years, and this three and a half year constitutes my first term. The wise custom that limits the President to two terms regards the substance and not the form. Under no circumstances will I be a candidate for or accept another nomination for the presidency."

On the cusp of his first full term, he instantly made himself a lame duck.

There was no statutory two-term limit at the time; it was a tradition going back to George Washington, who stepped down after his second term. When he made this announcement, his wife Edith, standing nearby, visibly flinched. Daughter Alice also heard the comment, *not quite believing her ears.*[xliii]

Later, he would say to a friend that *he would cut off his right hand if he could just take back those words.*

He would end up being haunted by that hasty pledge and hated the idea of giving up the presidency four years later, something he dearly loved.

He would spend years trying to win it back.[xliv]

Another television documentary expanded on the subject, featuring the historian Doris Kearns Goodwin, who said, "It was an impulsive gesture on the night he won the election. He made a mistake, perhaps, the biggest of his career. Boy, did he come to regret that."[xlv]

Of course, it's impossible to know how impulsive that decision may have been. We can never know how much he had thought it through as he approached election night. It struck him as honorable and in the tradition set by George Washington. But TR loved the presidency like no one else had. He reveled in it and making himself a lame duck didn't help him advance his policies either.

It's impossible to know the real reasons for the decision he made. As his statement said, it could have been fealty to the Washington two-term precedent, though TR wouldn't have served two full terms by the time of the 1908 election. Since he finished McKinley's term and would serve four years after being elected in 1904, it would have been easy to justify running again, serving two full terms of his own.

It may have been a deeply felt concern that he wouldn't outlive his father, who died at 46, and needed to devote himself to his burgeoning family. Given his love for the presidency and being the center of action and the country's attention, his decision is hard to understand.

Whatever the reason, Roosevelt felt honor-bound to stick by his announcement, though he would spend much of his remaining life trying to undo it.

Theodore Roosevelt had developed a close, personal relationship with William Howard Taft, long before he became president. That relationship continued when Taft became TR's secretary of war, a position he held for more than four years. As Roosevelt approached the end of what he described as his second term, it became apparent to all observers that Taft was his chosen successor.

Taft, on the other hand, never aspired to the presidency and would have preferred to be appointed to the Supreme Court. But his close friendship with Roosevelt led him to accept the passing of the torch for the 1908 presidential election.

Roosevelt's commitment to Taft was amply demonstrated in June 1908 as he engineered the nomination of the Republican Party for Taft. He "had to make fanatic Rooseveltians understand that he would not accept a draft himself…difficult for them to believe and depressing for him to reiterate, since the certainty that he would be elected if nominated" seemed obvious.

To his credit and consistent with the sense of honor he maintained, Roosevelt worked hard behind the scenes to secure Taft's nomination though it had to be difficult for him to do so.[xlvi]

Biographer Edmund Morris described the accomplishments of Theodore Roosevelt's 7-1/2-year presidency about as well as has been written. The "most powerfully positive American leader since Abraham Lincoln," and his record was substantial.

TR was "happy at the large things he had managed to achieve – a canal, a coal-strike settlement, a peace treaty, a national conservation conference – contented with myriad smaller triumphs, proud of his appointees, passionate about his country, in love with his wife and children; many-friended, much-honored, lusty in his physical and intellectual appetites, constantly bubbling with mirth; happy, above all, at having kept his promise not to hold on too long to power."[xlvii]

In the preface to Doris Kearns Goodwin's magnificent book about Roosevelt and Taft, *The Bully Pulpit*, she describes the Roosevelt presidency in the following manner:

"There are but a handful of times in the history of our country when there occurs a transformation so remarkable that a molt seems to take place, and an altered country seems to emerge. The turn of the twentieth century was such a time, and Theodore Roosevelt is counted among our greatest presidents, one of the few to attain that eminence without having surmounted some pronounced national crisis – revolution, war, widespread national depression."[xlviii]

H.G. Swells wrote that he seemed "a very symbol of the creative will in man." From Henry Adams: "Roosevelt, more than any other man living within the range of notoriety, showed the singular primitive quality that belongs to ultimate matter – the quality that medieval theology assigned to God – he was pure act."

His achievements would include: "the Monroe Doctrine reaffirmed, the Old World banished from the New World, the great Canal being cut; peace established in the Far East; the Open Door swinging freely in Manchuria and Morocco; Cuba liberated (and returned to self-government just in time for his departure); the Philippines pacified; the Navy hugely strengthened, known literally around the world; the Army, shorn of its old deadwood generals, feeling the green sap of younger replacements; capital and labor balanced off, the lynch rate declining, the gospel of cleaner politics now actually gospel and enough progressive principles established, or made part of the national debate, to keep legislative reformers busy for at least ten years."

And, in the minds of millions of Americans alive at the time, "he was already memorialized in the eighteen national monuments and five national parks he had created by executive order or cajoled out of Congress. The 'inventory', as Gifford Pinchot would say, included protected pinnacles, a crater lake, a rain forest and a petrified forest, a wind cave and a jewel cave, cliff dwellings, a cinder cone and skyscraper of hardened magma, sequoia stands, glacier meadows, and the grandest of all canyons."[xlix]

As he prepared to leave the presidency in 1908, he told William Jennings Bryan that, "I will confess to you that I like my job. The burdens…will be laid aside with a good deal of regret."[l]

After he left the presidency, entrusted to his close friend, William Howard Taft, TR grew increasingly restless about what he perceived as a conservative streak in the Taft presidency. The distance that developed in their relationship began to show itself at the time of Taft's inaugural.

There is probably nothing Taft could have done to satisfy Roosevelt short of turning over the office to him. There is no way TR would ever be satisfied; it now appears obvious.

During Taft's presidency, Roosevelt, as was typical, remained busy. In less than three weeks, after Taft's inauguration, he embarked on a year-long trip to Africa. Expecting to return to the United States from Khartoum, he was instead diverted to launch a six-week tour of the capitals of Europe in response to invitations from sovereigns across the globe.

Visiting Austria, Belgium, Denmark, England, France, Germany, Holland, Hungary, Italy, and Norway, he sailed home and received a tumultuous reception by a massive New York crowd. It was a fitting tribute after similar greetings that he experienced across Europe.[li]

Soon after his arrival home, he began a three-week, 16-state tour across the United States, making speech after speech and resembling a political candidate.

When Roosevelt announced his *New Nationalism* in a speech in the late summer of 1910 during that tour, he showed the public that his own thinking had moved far to the left and he was even more reform-minded than he had been as president.

It was disturbing for Taft because he saw a Roosevelt who was not only advocating far-reaching progressive measures that went well beyond anything he had done as president, but was clearly carving out a leadership role for himself.

Theodore Roosevelt would agree that his decision to make himself a lame duck on election night 1904 was a bad one. His actions after leaving the presidency demonstrated that he would make another bad decision which would damage many of the progressive causes that he so ably championed.

Theodore Roosevelt – Courtesy the Library of Congress

Bad Decision #2

William Howard Taft loved Theodore Roosevelt. There is no question about that, and it was something he expressed repeatedly during their long relationship. TR had also made it clear that he loved Taft, engineering Taft's ascension to the White House even though Taft never aspired to go there.

He once described his successor by saying, "He has the most lovable personality I have ever come in contact with."[lii]

But through his actions, Roosevelt showed that he loved himself even more; finding it impossible to observe Taft's presidency from afar, from being supportive, from making any attempt to retire graciously to the sidelines.

One of Roosevelt's biographers, Henry F. Pringle, wrote that "Self-control was a virtue expounded and admired by Roosevelt. But never, from the start of his public career, had he been able to turn a deaf ear to the Lorelei song of politics. He always shifted his course when the song drifted toward him. He always ignored, as he heard it, rocks and whirlpools and evil currents that threatened disaster."[liii]

Roosevelt and Taft were very different people, differing in a myriad of ways. Taft was never as ambitious as Roosevelt. Roosevelt changed his life at a young age through physical fitness, which remained a priority in his life until its end. Taft, on the other hand, was a large man, often of pale complexion and seriously overweight, ballooning to 320 pounds early in his presidency.

Taft's sport of choice was golf, something far too sedentary for TR. Roosevelt loved the presidency while Taft enjoyed the experience considerably less. Taft aspired not to be president but to be a member of the Supreme Court and looked at many of the problems in his administration from a legalistic standpoint. Roosevelt would approach problems only with activist solutions, often skirting the legalism that might be standing in his way.

Taft despaired as he watched his friend's performance during the late summer of 1910, with a full appreciation that a rupture in their friendship was brewing. He knew Roosevelt well and understood that TR wanted back in the White House, where Taft stood in his way.

As Goodwin wrote, "No matter how much he would rather be Will, welcoming his friend Theodore, he was now *President* Taft. 'I think, moreover, that [Roosevelt] will appreciate this feeling in me', he concluded, 'and would be the first one to resent the slightest subordination of the office of President to any man'."[liv]

Taft was a proud man who had not sought the presidency but, once there, took his responsibilities seriously, and did his level best. To watch the man, his most dear friend who had thrust him into that office acting out as he did was difficult. But even Taft couldn't foresee the path Roosevelt would take.

The Roosevelt presidency also dawned a new generation in journalism. Newspaper reporters covered TR assiduously and he provided them with access to the White House that had not previously existed. And he was good copy.

The country lapped up stories about Roosevelt, his family, and his exploits. The press coverage he enjoyed continued when he completed his worldwide voyage, also the source of tremendous accounts for American readers. So, when Roosevelt began to take issue with his successor, that also made good copy.

While Taft pledged to pursue tariff reform, something he considered critical, the press jumped on this departure from the Roosevelt administration. TR had avoided the issue to prevent a schism in the Republican Party. One of Roosevelt's close allies in his administration was Chief Forester Gifford Pinchot. Pinchot was in a public dispute with Interior Secretary Richard Ballinger and Taft sided with Ballinger, angering TR and his allies.

But issue differences were secondary, seeming to be mere justifications. How could Roosevelt seek to take away the presidency from Taft unless he did so from policy differences? These differences were a mere smokescreen that masked the Roosevelt ambition.

There were also personal matters between the families that were simply petty. Roosevelt's daughters felt slighted by treatment during White House events they had been invited to, something they felt was their due because of their father's role in putting Taft where he was. Taft invited TR to the White House, but the invitation was declined, causing Taft to feel a coolness in their friendship for which he was not prepared.

During the 1910 election season, Roosevelt campaigned hard across the country. In New York, he energetically sought to defeat changes in some of the progressive measures he had won as governor, efforts supported by the old-guard conservatives in the legislature. He traveled in many states to support progressive Republican candidates. When the results were in, Republicans were shocked by the Democratic gains.

Democrats won control of the House of Representatives, narrowed the margin of Republican control in the Senate, won 26 of 48 state governorships, and in New York, Roosevelt was humiliated. Whether or not Roosevelt held Taft responsible for the fortunes of progressive Republicans, the election outcome fueled his desire to get back into the ring.

In March 1911, Roosevelt embarked on a six-week trip throughout the South and Southwest, assuming it would be his last extensive speaking tour. But the crowds that greeted him at every stop were huge and enthusiastic. The press reported that rumors of his demise after the 1910 election debacle were greatly exaggerated. Roosevelt remained a force to be reckoned with.

During this same period, Wisconsin Senator Robert La Follette and other progressive leaders were forming an organization seeking to wrest control of the Republican Party from Taft and his more conservative supporters. They sought support from Roosevelt, but his response was tepid at best. La Follette saw himself as the best choice for the Republican nomination.

As conversations with Roosevelt continued throughout 1911, into the early months of the election year, supporters entreated TR to join their efforts with clear intimations that he pursue the nomination himself. He asserted that he would make no such effort to seek or secure the nod. But he was closer to doing just that than indicated.

When Michigan Governor Chase Osborn appealed to TR to run, claiming the support of at least a half-dozen Republican governors, Roosevelt told him if the pledges were in writing, he would announce his candidacy. Should he do that, he would have to first find a way to forestall the La Follette candidacy, which was growing in strength.

The Wisconsin senator bristled at those who were turning from him to the former president and refused to step aside. After a series of stumbles, his candidacy collapsed, and the progressive leaders turned once again to Roosevelt.[lv]

Taft was in a quandary. He felt that Roosevelt had long overshadowed his presidency *like a big, black cloud*. He hoped TR would ultimately decide not to run and was being told that Roosevelt's efforts were designed to get him to step aside. Taft had been an unhappy president and despaired at the possibility of open conflict with his old friend.

He felt that his chances to go onto the Supreme Court might be enhanced if he did step aside and Roosevelt returned to the office. But his sense of duty and dignity prevented him from doing so.

He told an associate, "I hate to be at odds with Theodore Roosevelt, who made me President...Of course, he made me *President* and not *deputy*, and I have to be President; and I do not recognize any obligation growing out of my previous relations to step aside and let him become a candidate for a third term when he specifically declined a third term."[lvi]

The die was cast with the two old friends now in opposition, each seeking the nomination of the Republican Party for president in 1912. As the campaign heated up, Roosevelt resorted to name-calling, referring to Taft as a *puzzlewit* and a *fathead*. Roosevelt was the clear winner in the primaries, besting Taft even in his own state of Ohio.

In addition to Ohio, TR won the states of Maryland, California, New Jersey, and South Dakota. Taft was the winner only in Massachusetts and New York, while La Follette captured North Dakota and his own state of Wisconsin.

The cumulative popular vote total was 1,214,969 for Roosevelt with Taft earning 865,835 votes to a lesser vote total for La Follette. But nominations are won in party conventions, and the incumbent president held a strong hand against the insurgent candidacy of the former president. Delegates choose nominees, not primary voters.

Described by William Jennings Bryan as "the most exciting ever held in the history of the country," the Republican National Convention of 1912 would, for the first time, pit two presidents against each other. The "bosom friends" had become "bitter enemies."[lvii] Held in Chicago, the Taft managers were firmly in control. Roosevelt's personal trip to Chicago and the speech he gave there raised the temperature for the delegates but changed little. Roosevelt told those watching his last speech of the nominating campaign that he decided to run because "Taft had definitely and completely abandoned the cause of the people and surrendered himself wholly to the biddings of the professional political bosses and the great privileged interests standing behind them." Nonetheless, William Howard Taft was nominated on the first ballot.

Former Senator Chauncey Depew was widely quoted as saying, "The only question now is which corpse gets the most flowers."[lviii]

Now, a decision was to be made. Would Roosevelt continue his mission to take the presidency away from Taft? No third-party candidate had ever won a national election but there had never been a Theodore Roosevelt either.

Soon, disgruntled progressive Republicans organized the new Progressive Party, and it didn't take long to procure a Roosevelt commitment to be their standard-bearer. The Democrats nominated another progressive, New Jersey Governor Woodrow Wilson, and the battle was on.

Another Roosevelt close friend would also part company over Roosevelt's campaign. Henry Cabot Lodge, a senator from Massachusetts, had forged a strong relationship with TR over several decades.

First becoming friends during the 1884 presidential election, they shared a vision for the nation and, during Roosevelt's presidency, would be allies against corporate power and political corruption.

Lodge had served in the House of Representatives for three terms before being elected to the Senate and was far better at forging alliances in Congress than TR would ever be. They formed a strong political partnership, sharing progressive goals; while Roosevelt led the progressive campaigns, Lodge would help make the president's goals a reality.

Lodge watched his friend's political activities prior to the 1912 Republican Convention with alarm. Roosevelt decided "to run as a crusading reformer who sought sweeping measures to combat the excesses of industrialization, Roosevelt joined progressive calls for referendums, the popular election of senators, and the recall of judicial opinions." Lodge didn't share TR's "insistence on participatory democracy" and felt the insurgent campaign against the Republican incumbent would only return the party to those forces outside the progressive movement.

Lodge preferred working within the constitutional framework and wouldn't allow himself to be part of an effort to bring down President Taft. It was a difficult decision for Lodge, but he was prescient. The Roosevelt campaign would have the effect on their shared progressive goals that he feared.[lix]

The Progressive Party became better known as the Bull Moose Party after TR's comment that he felt as fit as a bull moose. The election result was predictable, at least in part. A third-party candidacy normally impacts the candidate most closely aligned with it, meaning Roosevelt would take votes away from Taft.

What wasn't predictable was that Taft came in third, something unprecedented for an incumbent president. Wilson won overwhelmingly, winning 40 of 46 states and an electoral landslide of 435 electoral votes to Roosevelt's 88 (winning six states) and Taft's 8 (winning only Vermont and Utah).

Shortly after the election, President Taft was interviewed by a newspaper reporter, asking him if he thought Roosevelt would have entered the race if he had thought he'd destroy the Republican Party.

"I don't think he went deliberately into it that way," adding that Roosevelt was not, "a planner but simply a man who 'acts from day to day'." Sadly, late in the interview he added, "But Roosevelt was my closest friend."[lx]

The result of the Roosevelt candidacy in 1912 as head of the Progressive Party was to damage the progressive movement, particularly within the Republican Party. Members of his party lost elections across the country and his cause would have been better served by being fought within the two-party system than outside that system.

Roosevelt told Gifford Pinchot that "We must face the fact that our cutting loose from the Republican Party was followed by disaster to the progressive cause in most of the States where it won two years ago."[lxi]

Roosevelt didn't serve his own cause by running against Taft, quite the contrary. Honest reflection, perhaps years later, may have convinced him that his decision to run was not a good one. The poignant end to their relationship hints at this conclusion, that the rupture in their relationship caused by Roosevelt's activities was regretted by both.

They were reunited in 1918 during a chance meeting at a Chicago hotel; the two old friends embraced warmly, "like a pair of happy schoolboys." TR said to Taft, "I don't mind telling you how delighted I am," later adding, "I never felt happier in my life."[lxii]

The reunion meant so much to both men that Roosevelt had to have serious regrets about his Bull Moose campaign.

Within a year, Theodore Roosevelt was dead, dying in his sleep.

Vice President Thomas Marshall remarked that, "Death had to take him sleeping, for if Roosevelt had been awake, there would have been a fight."

Roosevelt had also reconciled with Henry Cabot Lodge, a man whom TR described *as his closest friend, personally, politically, and in every other way.* His eulogy at Roosevelt's funeral lasted all of two hours.[lxiii]

A tearful Taft attended the funeral, later saying to Roosevelt's sister, "I want to say to you how glad I am that Theodore and I came together after that long painful interval. Had he died in a hostile state of mind toward me, I would have mourned the fact all my life. I loved him always and cherished his memory."[lxiv]

Former President Taft would finally receive what he had always desired, an appointment to be chief justice of the Supreme Court. Appointed by President Warren Harding in 1921, he would serve there for nine years, widely admired and respected for the job he did, an office he dearly loved. Resigning because of ill health in 1930, he passed away just a month after his retirement.

Roosevelt's decision not to run for a second full term had an enormous impact on the rest of his life as well as on the progressive movement, which he held dear. His decision not to run in 1908 was an unhappy one for him and fueled his determination to return to the presidency.

He destroyed his close friendship with Taft, damaged his own causes, and ushered the Democrat, Wilson, into the White House. From Theodore Roosevelt's standpoint, as well as those who followed him and supported his causes, these decisions were certainly bad ones.

Woodrow Wilson – Courtesy the Library of Congress

Woodrow Wilson – The League of Nations

Recent history has been examining the life of Woodrow Wilson through a different lens. He was America's 28th president, the first to be a PhD, and the second to be awarded the Nobel Peace Prize.

He had always been seen as one of the giants among our presidents, leading the nation during World War I, when America took its place among the world as its preeminent democracy and the great power that had ended the Great War. He championed the creation of a League of Nations, an idealistic attempt to end future wars.

But now, a more critical view sees him as a racist, with a deep-seated attitude that colored much of his presidency, influencing the way he ran the government during his two terms. Born in the Deep South, he never abandoned the racist views he adopted early in life, and they represented a pernicious influence over his public actions.

But he was also an intellectual of the first order, authoring several books and developing an expertise of Congress and governmental institutions. As president of Princeton University, he became famous and was elected to be New Jersey's governor. From there, he sought and won the presidency in 1912 and was re-elected in 1916.

A Democrat, he benefited from the political war within the Republican Party, which had held the presidency for the previous 16 years. That war was between former presidents Theodore Roosevelt and William Howard Taft, virtually handing the presidency to Wilson.

In many respects, he was a giant, though tarred by the racism he demonstrated. But he could also be stubborn and was usually certain about the rightness of his opinions, a stubbornness that led to the great tragedy of his life. He was also a critical player in peace negotiations after the Great War. The Versailles Treaty, in which he played an important role, laid the groundwork for World War II in the way it punished Germany.

As the victorious powers extracted much from the German people, their subsequent suffering led to the rise of Adolph Hitler.

What would become known as World War I began in June 1914, with what may have appeared to be a fairly insignificant incident. Archduke Franz Ferdinand, the heir to the Austro-Hungarian throne was assassinated. Austria-Hungary held the nation of Serbia responsible and declared war.

Russia came to Serbia's defense and because of a myriad of defense alliances among the European nations, the nations of Germany, France, Great Britain, and the Ottoman Empire were drawn into the conflict. By November, it was truly a World War.

Wilson ran for re-election in 1916 as the candidate who had avoided becoming part of the World War. *He kept us out of war* was a popular slogan during the campaign. He was re-elected but it wasn't long before events forced the United States into the conflict as well. In April 1917, the U.S. declared war, largely because of German attacks against American shipping, plus a clumsy German attempt to compel Mexico to make war on its northern neighbor.

The American entry into the war tilted the balance firmly toward the Allied Powers and helped push the conflict to its end. It can be debated whether the American role was critical to the victory or not, but America's image in the world as well as among its own people changed because of the war and the victory.

The casualties suffered by the various nations were far worse than those suffered by the United States. Approximately 116,000 American soldiers were killed, with casualties totaling about 320,000. Of the Allied Powers, Britain suffered the deaths of 885,000 soldiers and France lost 1.4 million. Russia lost over 1.8 million and the Central Powers (Germany, Austria-Hungary, Bulgaria, and the Ottoman Empire) lost over 4 million soldiers.

Overall, the war cost close to 10 million soldiers dead with more than 21 million wounded. When civilian casualties are added in, through death, "disease, famine massacres, and collateral damage, somewhere between 16,500,000 and 65,000,000 people died – 1.75 percent of the population of the participating nations."[lxv]

By comparison, American losses were minuscule, but the role played by the United States in the aftermath was anything but. Wilson took the opportunity to step into a leadership role in attempting to frame a peace treaty.

The peace negotiations began before the fighting stopped, though the Allied victory appeared certain.

Wilson studied the various proposals from Allied leaders and sat down in January 1918 to write his own ideas on how peace should be constructed. These were his "Fourteen Points," and he went before Congress to make his case.

Wilson biographer A. Scott Berg wrote that, "A single theme ran through the text – what Wilson would describe as 'the principle of justice to all peoples and nationalities, and their right to live on equal terms of liberty and safety with one another, whether they be strong or weak'."

He told Congress that "We entered this war because violations of right had occurred which touched us to the quick and made the life of our own people impossible unless they were corrected and the world secured once for all against their recurrence. What we demand…is that the world be made fit and safe to live in."[lxvi]

Of the Fourteen Points, the first five "were *edicts for all nations to obey*: 'open *covenants* of peace, openly arrived at, absolute freedom of navigation upon the seas, the removal, so far as possible, of all economic barriers and an equality of trade conditions among all the nations *consenting* to the peace;' a reduction of national armaments 'to the lowest point consistent with domestic safety'; and 'A free, open-minded, and absolutely impartial adjustment of all colonial claims'."

The next eight points eradicated the old imperial borders of specific territories and entreated the rest of the world to honor the new boundaries.[lxvii] They dealt with a great deal of precision, defining very specific details affecting several nations, a Wilsonian drawing of a new European map.

The 14th point was for a League of Nations:

"A general association of nations must be formed under specific covenants for the purpose of affording mutual guarantees of political independence and territorial integrity to great and small states alike."[lxviii]

The League would be an international body, designed to bring nations together to discuss their differences and to be able to take steps that might avoid armed conflict.

While most world leaders applauded the Fourteen Points, Britain worried about how the second point would impact their ability to rule the waves as they always had.

French Premier Georges Clemenceau sarcastically remarked that "God was satisfied with Ten Commandments. Wilson gives us fourteen."

As the war wound down toward its end in November 1918, Wilson had to face a political reality at home. Despite his best efforts, the 1918 mid-term election was a Republican repudiation of the president. Both houses of Congress went Republican and Wilson faced a hostile Congress. Republican leaders like Theodore Roosevelt and Henry Cabot Lodge had spoken loudly against the Fourteen Points and urged Republican senators to reject them.

Roosevelt said, "such a peace would represent not the unconditional surrender of Germany but the conditional surrender of the United States."[lxix]

Those efforts, coupled with the flu epidemic that killed more than half a million Americans, affected American voters, many of whom were afraid to go to the polls fearing the virus.

The ultimate failure of the United States to ratify the League was largely due to Wilson's unwillingness to compromise. Insisting on the manner and form of the League, he barnstormed the nation, leading to a stroke that nearly ended his life and certainly ended his presidency.

Wilson was confident of his intellect and his sense of morality. "Nations and their leaders, Wilson believed, were subject to the political morality that was natural in individual men. When a leader made a decision for a whole people, he did so 'at the risk of the integrity of his own soul'. Legal rights…were secondary to ethics and the dictates of dedicated consciences." Wilson considered a nation to be *a moral essence*. He considered America to be a country established with a mission enunciated by the Declaration of Independence and the Bill of Rights. He saw leaders as having extralegal rights that went beyond the boundaries of law.

He had said, "I will not cry *peace* so long as there is sin and wrong in the world."

He felt it was the nation's destiny to "show other nations 'a fortunate way to happiness', to 'go to the ends of the earth carrying conscience and the principles that make for good conduct'."[lxx]

He felt strongly that the Anglo-Saxon peoples were the natural leaders for a world desperately needing moral leadership. Whether those views were also influenced by his feelings about non-whites are unknown, but he clearly held patronizing views about other, less well-developed nations, especially those without a democratic form of government. He saw America's responsibility to bring morality to these nations, even by force, as fully legitimate. His messianic impulses fueled his efforts to make the treaty a reality and his deep-seated racism colored his patronizing view of the nations led by non-whites.

While president of Princeton, he had suffered setbacks when trying to implement policy, setbacks that might have been avoided by someone more willing to compromise. One of Wilson's biographers, Arthur Walworth, wrote that "The stormy session of Congress, in the winter of 1915, revealed that the flaw in character that had led to Wilson's defeat at Princeton still remained, more dangerous than ever. Shrinking into personal isolation, indulging in dreams of the ideal government, and giving way to intolerance of the hard realities of politics, he had lost touch with seven important Democratic senators. His fury at them was so great that he wrote out a damning indictment that, fortunately, he was persuaded not to release. His friends wondered whether he had indeed cured himself, as he boasted in a talk to the Presbytery of Potomac, of the 'very risky habit of always saying exactly what he thought' – a trait that he said he had in part 'inherited' from his father."[lxxi]

The Louisville *Courier-Journal*, at one point, described him by writing that, "Woodrow Wilson is a schoolmaster rather than a statesman."[lxxii]

Wilson considered America's motives for entering the war and trying to manage the peace to be unselfish. His opponents saw him surrendering American sovereignty and bristled at his failure to advise and consent with the Senate. Wilson saw the opposition as choosing politics over humanitarianism.

His commitment to trying to shape the peace treaty led him to travel to Paris twice, returning between trips in order to take care of presidential responsibilities. It has been speculated that he had a stroke while in Paris or perhaps the flu, which seemed to be everywhere. There is some evidence that he experienced early symptoms of dementia.

Whatever the case, his health was poor and presented a challenge to go along with the challenges that other Allied leaders presented.

French Prime Minister Clemenceau, for instance, once remarked about the American president that Wilson "thought himself another Jesus Christ come upon the earth to reform men."[lxxiii]

To Wilson's credit, he warned his fellow leaders that they couldn't afford to punish Germany in a way that would force its people to rise up in revenge. Nonetheless, possibly due to his ill health, he gave in to the Allies' most punitive measures against Germany. And when a proposal was advanced that the treaty should provide for religious equality as well as racial equality, Wilson and his associates knew the Senate would never ratify "any Covenant which enshrined so dangerous a principle." This president, who had his White House show a motion picture for the first time, D.W. Griffith's *Birth of a Nation*, a movie that glorified the role of the Ku Klux Klan during Reconstruction, would never consider such a proposal. He spoke of a fear of Communism creeping into America because of "the American negro returning from abroad." He described the way "the French placed their Negro soldiers shoulder to shoulder with the whites. That concept, Wilson said, 'has gone to their heads'. For all his talk of evenhandedness, Wilson did not consider the races fundamentally equal, and he had no intention equalizing them under the law."[lxxiv]

This racist attitude was consistent with various actions in his presidency. He allowed his cabinet secretaries to "try to introduce segregation into the federal workplace, and he permitted them to reduce the number of African Americans employed by the government." For much of his presidency, he tried to ignore racial problems and was very much like a "great majority of white northerners of his time" in wishing that they would simply go away.[lxxv]

The Treaty of Versailles ended up comprising 440 articles. The first article was the League Covenant, an aspiration that there might be a means to avoid future conflicts like the one the world had just experienced. Subsequent articles dealt with less aspiration and more specifics. The treaty redrew Germany's boundaries, stripped Germany of its overseas possessions, and forced the dismantling of its military, its armaments as well as the size of its army and navy.

It redrew the boundaries of Austria-Hungary and the Ottoman Empire and required German reparations that began with a down payment of one million pounds. Further costs from the war would be assessed later. It was obvious to many of the victorious powers that the punitive measures were sowing the seeds for future conflict, but the Allied Powers moved ahead regardless.

Where cooler heads might have argued for the rehabilitation of the defeated powers, punishment was chosen instead. Despite the German objections, they had few choices before them; sign or continue the war.[lxxvi]

Wilson biographer John Milton Cooper, Jr. wrote that "the liberal program Wilson embraced that led to the Germans suing for peace in November 1918 rather than fighting on to the bitter end, as they would do a quarter of a century later" was "Wilson's greatest triumph. He shortened World War I, and hundreds of thousands, perhaps, millions of people owed their lives to him."[lxxvii]

Clearly, there were prominent leaders who saw in Wilson a level of principle and morality that they might find hard to see in others. Three years after Wilson's death, future British Prime Minister Winston Churchill declared, "Writing with every sense of respect, it seems no exaggeration to pronounce that the action of the United States with its repercussions on the history of the world depended, during the awful period of Armageddon, on the workings of this man's mind and spirit to the exclusion of every other factor; and that he played a part in the fate of nations incomparably more direct and personal than any other man."[lxxviii]

Wilson was treated like a conquering hero in Europe but returned to the United States as anything but. He understood that serious opposition existed to the treaty and was a seasoned politician who understood that he needed the Senate to ratify the treaty if it were to become law.

How he approached that opposition was an unnecessary and unforced error for which the president and the nation would pay a high price. The fact that this man, who typified the *my way or the highway* mentality, succeeded in politics as he did is somewhat amazing. But that mentality would provide the seeds for his ultimate failure.

His didactic approach toward members of Congress created some intense feelings. Massachusetts Senator Henry Cabot Lodge, who had been the Republican leader in the Senate before he assumed the chairmanship of the foreign relations committee, was a dangerous opponent for Wilson to have.

And when Wilson sought ratification of the Versailles Treaty, which was required by the Senate, an alliance with Lodge would have served Wilson's interest. Instead, he fostered the most negative feelings from Lodge, who was also close to Theodore Roosevelt, another political figure who held negative views about Wilson. Lodge considered Wilson "an overbearing egotist and dictator," later writing to Roosevelt that "I never expected to hate anyone in politics with the hatred I feel towards Wilson."[lxxix]

Here was a president who had authored a book about Congress, and who clearly understood the requirements of politics at the level in which he served. He felt strongly that the Versailles Treaty was right and just. His commitment to the League of Nations was sincere and intense. Yet he did not seek a way to work with Congress to make these views prevail.

Instead, he decided to reach over the heads of Congress and go directly to the American people, campaigning energetically soon after returning to the United States after a grueling period of treaty negotiations in Paris and major threats to his health.

Was that approach necessary? Could he have successfully dealt with Congress? One of Wilson's biographers, A. Scott Berg, wrote about Senator Lodge being considered to be named chair of the Peace Commissioners Wilson was appointing. "His well-known enmity toward the President kept anybody from seriously considering the idea, though pundits ever since have suggested that if chosen, he would have ensured passage of the Treaty."[lxxx]

Perhaps, a more pragmatic leader would have brought Lodge on board for the greater good – or at least tried.

It was also suggested to the president that he convene the leaders in the war effort from both sides of the political spectrum to the East Room in the White House, a conference in which he would "imbue them with a sense of personal gratitude and then say 'that the worst and hardest was yet to come…in the readjustment of the world', and 'that their cooperation, their loyalty to the country, and to the great cause, will even be more needed then than it was during the war'."

Wilson was encouraged to do this as a way to suppress party opposition and his well-known persuasiveness would carry the day. Wilson "never acted upon the idea, and antagonism festered."[lxxxi]

Harold Nicholson, a British member of its delegation at the Peace Conference, wrote the following about Wilson. Describing his "one-track mind," he added: "The intellectual disability rendered him blindly impervious, not merely to human character, but also shades of difference. He possessed no gift for differentiation, no capacity for adjustment to circumstances. It was his spiritual and mental rigidity which proved his undoing. It rendered him as incapable of withstanding criticism as of absorbing advice. It rendered him blind to all realities which did not accord with his preconceived theory, even to the realities of his own decisions."[lxxxii]

Wilson felt that the United States had entered the war to change the world and keep wars from happening and that the American people would see the wisdom in the treaty and the League as well. But it wasn't as simple as that.

One of Wilson's closest friends and advisors throughout his presidency was Colonel Edward House. They were so close that Wilson once said, "Mr. House is my second personality. He is my independent self. His thoughts and mine are one."[lxxxiii]

That relationship was strained to breaking when Wilson left Paris after his first trip there, leaving House in charge of ongoing negotiations. When Wilson returned to Paris and rejected virtually all that House had done, the relationship was broken.

Each man felt rejected by the other. In their last conversation, as Wilson was preparing to return home, House "urged Wilson to return to the Senate in a conciliatory spirit, one of 'consideration' instead of confrontation. 'House', the President replied, 'I have found one can never get anything in this life that is worthwhile without fighting for it'. House disagreed, extolling the virtues of compromise and contending, 'that a fight was the last thing to be brought about, and then only when it could not be avoided'. Those would be the last sentences the two would ever exchange in person, as the President chose never to see him again."[lxxxiv]

Wilson returned from France to a country that looked far different than when he made his first trip across the ocean. The country had mobilized for war as it should have and that changed America in many ways. But the demobilization after the war's end changed the country in far different ways.

The war and its end brought on massive inflation, with prices in America doubling between the beginning of Wilson's first term and the end of the war. Labor unrest was percolating across the nation; it would be unpatriotic for unhappy workers to strike while the nation was at war. Racial unrest was rising in many parts of the country, exacerbated by returning black vets who found it hard to return to the Jim Crow laws after fighting for their country.

A post-war recession added to the unsettled country and the level of national dissatisfaction rose. Add to that, the Republicans were now in control of the Senate, where Wilson's treaty would have to be approved.[lxxxv]

The president didn't focus on the inflation or the unrest among laborers or blacks. Instead, he was laser-focused on passing the treaty. His most optimistic vote count for ratification in the Senate was that he was only two votes short. But a head-to-head vote wouldn't take place as long as the chairman of the Senate foreign relations committee wanted to delay consideration and offer amendments.

Wilson faced a decision. Could he consider amendments or any measure of compromise with Sen. Lodge? Was it possible to win the votes he needed among undecided senators or those opponents who could be pressured to change their votes by appealing directly to the American electorate? Woodrow Wilson could not countenance compromise on the League of Nations even if other matters in the treaty might be up for discussion. And it was the League that Lodge and the other opponents concentrated on.

Therefore, Wilson decided to take his case to the country as a way to persuade the Senate. There was no history serving as a precedent for such an effort, little reason to feel that this approach could succeed. Nonetheless, Wilson launched an aggressive campaign to take the issue of the treaty to the public and to the voters. He and his staff outlined a four-week trip of greater than 10,000 miles with stops in 29 cities, all but four of the states west of the Mississippi.[lxxxvi]

President and Mrs. Wilson left Washington with their entourage on September 3, 1919. The First Lady Edith Wilson was gravely concerned about her husband's health well before he launched this latest journey. She had witnessed his array of illnesses while in Europe and saw that he looked gray and pale in the days before leaving the capitol. She had to have been amazed by the energy Wilson was able to show during his trip across the country, giving speech after speech, seemingly growing stronger by the effort, being heard by thousands of Americans every day. But Wilson's energy failed him when he suffered a massive stroke about three weeks into his journey.

The entourage canceled the remaining commitments and brought the ailing president home. Then a new ordeal began, as Edith Wilson protected the president from every possible stress. He could do no work nor be seen by any of his cabinet members or the vice president. Only a handful of aides and his doctor were allowed access to the president by his wife.

Official Washington was being told that the president's body was broken but his mind remained healthy and strong. Yet, a "month passed during which no government official, not even a secretary, saw the President of the United States. Nobody even shaved him."[lxxxvii]

A month after his return to the White House, Wilson's health reeled from better to worse, and when the former, carefully choreographed visits were allowed for selected officials and various guests. The longer he remained absent, the more his Senate opponents realized that they were in charge, that they could do away with the entire treaty if they chose to. Dozens of modifications were agreed to even though they knew Wilson would probably accept none of them. When Wilson was up to discussing the Senate's actions with the occasional visitor, it was clear that he was still unwilling to compromise. By the time the Senate neared adjournment at the end of the year, it was hopelessly deadlocked, and the treaty could not pass.

To protect her husband further, Edith Wilson banned the public from the White House and its grounds. When the vice president tried to visit the president, he was denied entry. Wilson's absence led to constant rumors; he had died, he had lost his mind, and on and on. The open question before the country, and history, concerned who was in charge. Was Edith, in fact, the de facto president?

Cabinet members wondered whether it was appropriate for an incapacitated president to run the country. The constitution had gaps in it that failed to specifically determine a process for presidential inability and succession, gaps that wouldn't go away until the passage of the 25th Amendment in 1967, during a time when it was far more dangerous to have presidential inability than it was in 1919.

Nonetheless, it appears clear that the real power of decision-making was left in the hands of the First Lady. The fact that the president was not in charge led to disarray in the White House and the cabinet with several departures due to what was an intolerable situation. In the words of biographer, A. Scott Berg, "With another year to his term, Woodrow Wilson became the lamest duck ever to inhabit the White House, residing more than presiding for the rest of his days there."[lxxxviii]

George Reedy, a former press secretary in Lyndon Johnson's White House wrote about Wilson and this failed effort. "Wilson castigated the 'little group of willful men' in the Senate who, he believed, had wrecked his grand design for world peace through American participation in the League of Nations. In the light of subsequent events, Wilson may have been right in his predictions of dire consequences should our country refuse to enter the League…An objective student of the period, though, must admit that the voters simply were not ready for the step at the time. It was the American people – not the Senate – who frustrated the president."[lxxxix]

The decision by Woodrow Wilson to take his case to the country rather than seek accommodations with the Senate doomed not only the Versailles

Treaty and the League of Nations but doomed him as well. Perhaps, a compromise wouldn't have worked; there may have been no way to accommodate Henry Cabot Lodge and the treaty's Senate opponents.

But the solution sought by Wilson certainly didn't work and he ended up a shell of a man and the treaty died along with his presidency. Perhaps, the League of Nations or a different sort of treaty would have forestalled the coming Second World War.

We cannot know for sure. Perhaps. a different sort of man with different prejudices and rigidity would have been more successful than Wilson. But it is possible the idealistic solutions he sought at the war's end wouldn't have been created had it not been for a man like him.

Whatever the case, it's hard to view this presidential decision as a good one.

Franklin D. Roosevelt – Courtesy Franklin D. Roosevelt Presidential Library

FDR – The Internment of Japanese Americans

Americans are racist.

That statement can launch a vigorous argument in many parts of the United States. But whether we are racists or not, there are several episodes in American history when racial prejudice led to shameful, national behavior.

The most obvious examples begin with slavery, the enslavement of Africans, kidnapped from their homeland and brought to our shores to serve white masters. Then, there were the Indian wars, the result of Native Americans resisting the encroachment of their lands by white settlers.

Racial prejudice is not rational but there are often rationalities that are used to make the racially prejudiced events seem justified. African Americans were seen as lesser humans, making slavery seem acceptable. Native Americans were killing white settlers, making their massacre seemingly justified. And, of course, there is anti-Asian prejudice as well as anti-Semitism.

These examples were not just episodes of prejudice by certain individuals but were enabled by law. And many American leaders, by their own behavior, endorsed these traditions by owning slaves or taking part in the removal of the Indians from their native lands. Were some of our presidents racist? That is hard to dispute; many were, in fact, slaveholders. History has also shown that there were more than 1,800 members of the House and Senate who owned slaves.[xc]

But Franklin Delano Roosevelt was not a racist. While a patrician from a Hyde Park estate in New York, he showed a great deal of empathy for his fellow citizens of all races and creeds. Perhaps, it was the paralysis he suffered from polio and the rehabilitation he sought in Warm Springs, Georgia, a locale populated by others afflicted by polio or debilitating injuries. Maybe it was the familiarity with a myriad of races and ethnicities he gained by his immersion in New York politics.

His presidency demonstrated many examples of empathy and protection of minorities, and he was beloved by African Americans across the land. Whatever the case, it is hard to view his life and career as one marked by racist behavior. When anti-Jewish measures were being enacted in Nazi Germany, he spoke out against anti-Semitism. In fact, he appointed more Jews to important posts in his administration than ever before.

However, he agreed to the internment of Japanese Americans in concentration camps after the Japanese attack on Pearl Harbor, leading the United States into war.

This was not a knee-jerk decision made in a time of crisis. There was a long, historical lead-up to the steps that FDR and the American government made to lock away American citizens during World War II. Long before the attack on Pearl Harbor, the United States had developed plans to deal with alien residents should a war come from foreign adversaries.

The legal basis for the steps taken in the 1930s as the build-up toward war began was the Alien Enemies Act of 1798. It provided the basis for the FBI's process to compile lists of American residents who were born in nations hostile to the United States.

In that period, nationals from Japan, Germany, and Italy were targeted. As tensions with Japan increased late in the decade, particular attention was paid to the Japanese immigrants in Hawaii, an area deemed vulnerable to a Japanese attack. [xci]

Ironically, the Japanese attack against the United States was itself, at least in part, the result of racism on the international stage. Japan had been one of the nations present at Versailles to negotiate the treaty ending World War I. Yet its diplomats were universally ignored by the international leaders.

And as Japan sought to expand its possessions in the Pacific in the years between the wars, enlarging its empire as Britain, Portugal, the Dutch, and the Americans had done, extreme sanctions were brought against it. Japanese leaders bristled at the double standard being practiced by the other nations. The sanctions also restricted the ability of the Japanese to acquire various natural resources available in the Pacific that they had previously depended on. They made war against nations in the Pacific in order to secure these resources.

On August 10, 1936, President Roosevelt proposed to the chief of naval operations that "every Japanese citizen or non-citizen on the island of Oahu who meets these Japanese ships (arriving in Hawaii) or has any connection with their officers or men should be secretly but definitely identified and his or her name placed on a special list of those who would be the first to be placed in a concentration camp in the event of trouble."

Such a system was created by the military and the FBI was enlisted to develop a list of those who would fall under suspicion. Three categories were created. Group A included those considered most dangerous, especially those who were members of Communist or fascist organizations as well as German, Italian, or Japanese organizations. Group B was for those less dangerous but still active in religious or cultural organizations that might lead them to share the values of the hostile nations. Group C included a wider array of people who might be considered suspicious for a variety of reasons. As it turned out, the number of people considered dangerous, even in Group A, was quite small.[xcii]

However, there were 1.2 million American residents born in Germany and five million had two German-born parents. Those who were of similar Italian heritage were a part of an even larger group. During the war, the government incarcerated about 11,500 persons of German ancestry and another 3,000 of Italian ancestry.

We now know that the Germans sent spies into the United States, and it was something the public was fearful of during these years. But neither Germans nor Italians experienced the broad and sweeping incarcerations that were experienced by Japanese Americans and their parents. [xciii]

Those areas of the country considered most vulnerable to pro-Japanese espionage were the West Coast states and Hawaii. In the 80 years prior to the war, nearly 275,000 Japanese immigrated to the United States, a large percentage settling in Hawaii with the incentive being available jobs in the sugarcane fields.

Congress passed the Chinese Exclusion Act in 1882; the first time the American government had ever denied entry into the country to any people. The Chinese Exclusion Act was signed by President Chester Arthur, totally barring the immigration of Chinese laborers. The United States passed a number of other laws over the years that discriminated directly against Asian immigrants.

On the mainland, Japanese immigrants controlled less than 4% of California's farmland but it was estimated that they produced over 10% of the state's farm resources. That impressive level of production did not bring them appreciation from white Americans but seemed to generate resentment instead. They found it hard to purchase land under California law and would later find themselves unable to become citizens.[xciv]

In Hawaii, the influx of immigrants reduced the presence of native Hawaiians from 96% of the population in 1853 to approximately 25% by the end of the 19th century. Contract laborers were largely Chinese, Filipino, Korean, and Japanese, but the powers on the islands were definitely white.

In 1921, a white businessman in Honolulu, Walter Dillingham, stated, "When you are asked to go in the sun and into the canebrake away from the tropical breeze you are subjecting the white man to do something that the good Lord did not create him to do. If He had, the people of the world, I think, would have had a white pigment of the skin and not variegated colors."[xcv]

What was basically a plantation system in Hawaii fed into the prejudices about the non-whites who served the bosses. These attitudes became important as the nation reacted to the Japanese bombing of Pearl Harbor. But this was not restricted to Hawaii. In fact, this racial discrimination found its way into law by measures that refused citizenship to Japanese not born in the U.S.

In 1906, the Naturalization Act was passed, restricting the right of citizenship to immigrants. It was upheld by the Supreme Court in 1922 when challenged by an American resident, high school graduate, and former student at UC Berkeley. The Court ruled that his race, neither a *free white man* nor someone of African descent, precluded him from a right of citizenship.

In 1924, the Johnson-Reed Act, signed into law by President Calvin Coolidge, cut off any further immigration from Japan.[xcvi] It set immigration limits by country, favoring northern Europe over others. While white protestants were clearly prioritized, it effectively banned all Asians.

But it wasn't immigration that was impacted by the Japanese Americans who would be interned. The pros and cons of immigration laws can be argued but these people were already living in the United States.

When the war began, suspicions directed toward aliens were immediate. The dastardly and surprise attack perpetrated on December 7, 1941, led to immediate concerns about possible sabotage in the United States by residents who might be more loyal to Japan than the country they currently called home.

As war news seemed to be consistently bad, those who looked down on the Japanese Americans raised their voices the loudest. Newspaper cartoons often showed Japanese people as rats, insects, skinks, monkeys, lice, or rabid dogs. One cartoon strip, titled 'How to Spot a Jap', featured instructions for distinguishing between Japanese and Chinese Americans:

"A Jap is shorter and looks as if his legs are joined directly to his chest...The Jap has buck teeth...The Chinese strides, The Jap shuffles." Restaurant owners put signs in their front windows: THIS RESTAURANT POISONS BOTH RATS AND JAPS. When Jap didn't seem a degrading enough epithet, sign makers and cartoonists alike went with '*Nip* or *Yellow vermin*'. Some of the country's most influential editorial writers began to feel hatred. Talking about the American-born Nisei, the *Los Angeles Times* editorialized, 'A viper is nonetheless a viper wherever the egg is hatched'. Congressman John Rankin of Mississippi was quoted as saying, "This is a race war... I say it is of vital importance that we get rid of every Japanese... Damn them! Let's get rid of them now!" Congressman Jed Johnson of Oklahoma demanded the forced sterilization of all Japanese living in the United States while the governor of Idaho Chase Clark, said, "The Japs live like rats, breed like rats, act like rats."[xcvii]

Governor Clark, whose future son-in-law would be Idaho's four-term U.S. Senator Frank Church, opposed the Idaho internment camp and expounded upon his opinions of the Japanese Americans. "I realize we've got to put them some place, but I don't trust any of them." He suggested they all be sent back to Japan and *sink the island*.[xcviii]

Within a month after Pearl Harbor, in early 1942, the war department issued an order that Japanese Americans were not eligible to serve in the U.S. military. They would be classified under a new designation by draft boards, 4-C enemy aliens.[xcix]

February 1, 1942, President Roosevelt signed a memo to Secretary of War Stimson saying, "Americanism is not, and never was, a matter of race or ancestry. A good American is one who is loyal to this country and our creed of liberty and democracy. Every loyal American should be given the opportunity to serve this country."[c] On February 19, executive order 9066 was issued with region-specific exclusion orders and was accompanied by military curfew orders for all Japanese Americans.[ci] The order *authorized the forced removal of all persons deemed a threat to national security from the West*

Coast to relocation centers further inland – resulting in the incarceration of Japanese Americans. Civilians were excluded from military areas and, while the order did not specify which ethnic groups should be put under curfews, only Japanese Americans were subjected to them.

Congress unanimously enacted legislation authorizing the removal of Japanese Americans from the West Coast on March 21, 1941. The forced evacuation from their homes began right away. Those being evacuated were given 48 hours' notice, and between March and September 1942, 125,284 Japanese Americans, including men, women, and children, were moved to "assembly centers." From there, they were transported to "relocation centers," also referred to as "internment camps." There were 10 sites in remote areas of six states in the West plus Arkansas. The sites were Tule Lake and Manzanar in California, Minidoka in Idaho, Topaz in Utah, Colorado River Relocation Center (Granada), Poston and Gila River in Arizona, Heart Mountain in Wyoming, Jerome and Rohwer in Arkansas.

Approximately 70,000 of these evacuees were American citizens. Many others would have been citizens if the restrictions hadn't been enacted.

Those persons subjected to this incarceration were never charged with a crime and were allowed no process to appeal their incarceration. Not only were their personal liberties being taken away, but most lost their homes and significant amounts of personal property as well.[cii]

While Congress may have acted unanimously, the Roosevelt administration was far from unanimous.

Secretary of the Treasury Henry Morgenthau said that, "No one except Harold Ickes and myself could want to go further [in protecting the nation], but when it comes to suddenly mopping up a hundred and fifty thousand Japanese and putting them behind barbed wire," he needed "some time to catch my breath."

Ickes, the secretary of the Interior, was the administration's strongest advocate on civil rights and protecting civil liberties but even he understood at the commencement of the policy, that opposing it publicly would have caused considerable difficulties for him as well as for his colleagues.

Even the progressive U.S. Senator Hiram Johnson of California was a strong advocate of the internment policy and, with Navy Secretary Frank Knox, was "desperate to escape blame for December 7 by fingering what Roosevelt described as 'potential fifth columnists'." More than 125,000 people were "mopped up" and neither Ickes nor FBI director J. Edgar Hoover, who also opposed the internment, could "prevent Roosevelt from yielding to race-baiting political demands."[ciii]

Ickes argued with FDR about the internment and despite that, the president put him in charge of the War Relocation Authority, which oversaw the operation of the internment camps. He continued to press for an end to the policy, "labeling his opponents as wanting a 'lynching party'." And when hundreds of internees at the Tule Lake Segregation Center rioted, he had to talk Roosevelt down from a desire to crush the rioters, whom FDR considered mutineers.[civ]

As FDR faced a re-election campaign for an unprecedented fourth term, Ickes turned up the heat, fully realizing that the president would take no action prior to the election. Nevertheless, he wrote to the president, demanding an end to the internment orders, laying out his reasons: "imprisonment without trial was unconstitutional; it was no more a military necessity than martial law in Hawaii; and psychological damage was being wrought on Japanese-American children who were becoming a hopelessly maladjusted generation."[cv]

After two years of the incarceration, Interior Secretary Harold Ickes and First Lady Eleanor Roosevelt lobbied the president to resettle the refugees back to the West Coast. Roosevelt finally announced a new policy after securing his third re-election.

The incarceration program was ended and the people who had been held were free to go, to return to their homes or wherever they chose to resettle. The military situation in the war had changed and even the military supported the end of the evacuation orders.[cvi] Plus, there had been no acts of treachery by Japanese Americans as feared by American leaders when the program was instituted.

The prior year, the military created a Japanese American regiment, the Nisei, which had greatly distinguished itself in the European theater. The 442nd Regimental Combat Team made up of 18,000 Japanese American men, many of whom had been in the camps and still had families housed there, demonstrated disproportionate valor in the war.

Approximately 16 million Americans served in World War II, resulting in 473 Congressional Medals of Honor. The Nisei were awarded 21 of those commendations. The 442nd represented .11% of the military force but earned 4.4% of those medals. "Additionally, the regiment earned 29 Distinguished

Service Crosses, 560 Silver Stars, 28 Silver Stars with oak leaf clusters (in place of a second Silver Star), 22 Legion of Merit Medals, 4,000 Bronze Stars, 1,200 Bronze Stars with oak leaf clusters, 36 Commendation Medals, 87 Division Commendations, and more than 4,000 Purple Hearts."[cvii]

After the war, many of the country's leaders began to face up to the injustices suffered by Japanese Americans. President Truman made efforts to restore the property and civil rights of those who had suffered under his predecessor's policy. Writing to Eleanor Roosevelt, Truman said, "These disgraceful actions almost make you believe that a lot of our Americans have a streak of Nazi in them."

In 1948, he pushed the Japanese Americans Evacuation Claims Act through Congress. When speaking directly to the Nisei soldiers who had been part of the 442nd, he said, "You fought not only the enemy, but you fought prejudice – and you've won. Keep up that fight and we'll win."[cviii]

In 1952, Congress passed the McCarran-Walter Act, finally allowing Japanese immigrants to apply for citizenship. Over the ensuing decades, former Nisei soldiers lobbied Congress for a formal apology by the country as well as direct compensation to those families affected by the evacuation policy.

The government established the Commission on Wartime Relocation and Internment of Civilians and, three years later, the commission recommended a formal apology and the sought-after compensation. Those desires were finally satisfied by passage of the Civil Liberties Act of 1988, which President Reagan signed into law.[cix]

When 20 members of the 442nd Regiment were honored at the White House with the Medals of Honor in 2000, many posthumously, President Clinton stated, "Rarely has a nation been so well served by a people it has so ill-served."[cx]

It's easy to understand the pressures facing FDR as the war broke out. But it is not as easy to understand why he succumbed to these pressures as he did. His 12 years as president showed him to be a man who stood his ground many times against the advice of advisors, politicians, and the military. He was a man who knew his own mind and was comfortable standing alone with his decisions on many occasions.

Would he have come to regret these measures that trampled on the rights of American citizens and in a way that singled Japanese Americans out when descendants of our other enemies, Germany and Italy, were not so targeted? We can never know.

But a man like Franklin Roosevelt, a student of history and a great patriot, a man who not only lifted the nation out of a depression but successfully led his nation in the war brought on by foreign adversaries, cared about his legacy. It is hard to believe he would have wanted to be remembered as a president who singled out so many of his fellow citizens and those who resided in the country for such treatment.

And there is no evidence that the incarceration of Japanese Americans prevented a single act of espionage or disloyalty. But that was not so obvious when Pearl Harbor was attacked.

Perhaps Roosevelt was too preoccupied with the war in Europe. He saw Hitler as the personification of evil and understood that the American way of life depended on prevailing in that struggle against evil. The Japanese attack was insidious, a sneak attack on the American Navy, an institution FDR considered dear. As one of Roosevelt's biographers, Jean Edward Smith, wrote, "it is difficult to appreciate the implicit racial hostility toward Japan that characterized Roosevelt's discussions with his advisors as war drew near."[cxi]

Shortly after Pearl Harbor, there was scant concern about Japanese Americans living on the West Coast. But as it became clear how great the losses were by the Navy and how successfully Japan was conquering the South Pacific, the public began to show antagonism toward those Japanese living in the United States. It became easy to blame the devastation of the Pearl Harbor attack on "legions of saboteurs undermining resistance from within."[cxii]

Biographer Smith wrote, "The tipping point for public opinion came on January 24, 1942, when the Roberts Commission, which had been appointed by FDR to investigate the Pearl Harbor attack, reported that Nagumo's strike force had been aided by Hawaiian-based espionage agents, including American citizens of Japanese ancestry. The commission provided no evidence to substantiate the charge, but the remark was sufficient to unleash a torrent of anti-Japanese reaction. *The Los Angeles Times*, which as recently as January 23 had advised moderation, called on January 28 for the relocation of all Japanese living in the State whether they were citizens or not. Politicians jumped on the bandwagon. By the end of January, the entire California congressional delegation, as well as Democratic governor Culbert L. Olsen and

Republican attorney general Earl Warren, was clamoring for removal of the Japanese."*[cxiii]

Future Supreme Court Chief Justice Earl Warren, in his autobiography published in 1977, stated that he had been wrong. "I have since deeply regretted the removal order and my own testimony advocating it. Whenever I thought of the innocent little children who were torn from home, school friends, and congenial surroundings I was conscience-stricken. It was wrong to act so impulsively…even though we had a good motive." [cxiv]

The pressure to remove the Japanese Americans from their homes was intensified by the national press, including the legendary Walter Lippman and his more conservative colleague Westbrook Pegler. After the West Coast was declared a combat zone, Lippman wrote, "Nobody's constitutional rights include the right to reside and do business on a battlefield."[cxv]

There was a dispute between members of the Roosevelt administration and military leaders, the latter who didn't want troops assigned to administer an evacuation policy when they were greatly needed in Europe. Attorney General Francis Biddle, Secretary of War Henry Stimson, and Assistant Secretary of War John McCloy struggled with the constitutional issues yet shared a concern about domestic security on the West Coast.

Stimson wrote in his diary, "The second-generation Japanese can only be evacuated as part of a total evacuation, or by frankly trying to put them out on the ground that their racial characteristics are such that we cannot understand or trust even the citizen Japanese. This latter is the fact, but I am afraid it will make a tremendous hole in our constitutional system."[cxvi]

Internment had previously taken place in American history during World War I. Non-citizen German Americans were considered enemy aliens. Six thousand "suspected enemy aliens were interned or detained under presidential warrants for the duration of the war, along with 'several thousand more held for shorter periods'." J. Edgar Hoover, who had been an official in the Bureau of Investigation, which would later become the F.B.I., was very much involved with the internment then but came to oppose it as F.B.I. director during World War II. He saw how little positive impact it had had on the war effort compared to the very negative impact it had on the lives involved.[cxvii]

The Roberts Commission was headed by Supreme Court Justice Owen Roberts. Nagumo was Japanese Vice Admiral Chuichi Nagumo, the man assigned the task of planning the attack on Pearl Harbor.

Hoover's opinion was that Japanese Americans could be considered as individuals. But he was met with a response from one of the generals in charge that "A Jap is a Jap," and that none could be trusted. When Hoover joined Attorney General Biddle in proposing an administration statement that affirmed Japanese American loyalty and "rejecting the mass internment of citizens, the military men refused to sign and walked out."[cxviii]

The question was referred to the president. Secretary Stimson found FDR focusing on military matters and was told to do what he thought best. No opinion about the evacuation was expressed. The matter was delegated to Stimson, who turned it over to McCloy, who determined that military necessity justified the evacuation measures. The war department drafted the executive order and Roosevelt signed it.

Doris Kearns Goodwin described the internment of Japanese Americans as "an ill-advised, brutal decision" and added that "Racism fueled the claim of military necessity." Goodwin wrote about Eleanor Roosevelt's opposition to the policy. The former first lady later wrote that "These people were not convicted of any crime but emotions ran too high, too many people wanted to wreak vengeance on Oriental looking people. There was no time to investigate families or to adhere strictly to the American rule that a man is innocent until he is proven guilty." The orders for the evacuation "took her breath away. To her mind, the guarantees of the Bill of Rights must never be surrendered, even in the face of national disaster. When she tried to speak to her husband about his decision, however, he gave her a frigid reception and said he did not want her to mention it again."[cxix]

FDR later said he regretted "the burdens of evacuation and detention which military necessity imposed on these people." He did not live past the war's end to be able to reflect on these actions. His attorney general wrote, "I do not think he was much concerned with the gravity or implications of this step. He was never theoretical about things. What must be done to defend the country must be done. The military might be wrong. But they were fighting the war. Nor do I think that the constitutional difficulty plagued him – the Constitution has never greatly bothered any wartime President."[cxx]

James MacGregor Burns, in his Roosevelt biography, described Roosevelt's assistant Harry Hopkins as saying, "'Will it help to win the war?' but such a test was likely to ignore broader strategic aspects of winning the war – and the relation between winning the war and defending democracy." Burns also described the evacuation policy in this way: "To the military, this seemed a wise precaution, but in the long run it was a compromise with the ideas the nation was supposed to be fighting."[cxxi]

This treatment of Japanese Americans is a blight on the presidency of Franklin D. Roosevelt and his legacy. He may not have been a racist, but the internment policy shows a level of insensitivity, at the very least, that has not been part of his reputation or image.

Perhaps, it took the civil rights battles of later decades to make Americans see the internment policy properly, even though FDR's wife Eleanor and Harold Ickes saw it for what it was at the time. Many Americans suffered because of this policy and the legacy of Franklin Roosevelt suffers as well.

It was, indeed, a bad decision.

Bill Mauldin Cartoon – Copyrights held by and image courtesy of the Pritzker Military Museum & Library

Kennedy-Nixon Debate – Courtesy the Library of Congress

Richard M. Nixon Versus John F. Kennedy – To Debate or Not to Debate

The 1960 presidential campaign between Vice President Richard M. Nixon and Senator John F. Kennedy was a time of great generational change in America. They were the first presidential candidates born in the 20th century and either would be substantially younger than any president since Theodore Roosevelt.

The baby boomers born after World War II would just begin paying attention to national affairs as Kennedy and Nixon competed; each inspired a generation of young people to yearn for their own roles in American politics.

As different as they may have seemed to many Americans, there were also similarities. Four years apart in age, Nixon was born in 1913 and Kennedy in 1917, both were veterans of the recent World War. Kennedy, in fact, was renowned as a war hero. Each came to Congress at the same time, elected to the House of Representatives in 1946, and they became friendly with one another during those first years on Capitol Hill.

Both men aspired to higher office with Nixon getting himself elected to the U.S. Senate in 1950 and Kennedy doing the same two years later. But their backgrounds were very different.

Nixon had grown up in Whittier, California, the son of Quakers who struggled to make ends meet. Kennedy, on the other hand, was born into one of America's wealthiest families, Catholics from Boston, Massachusetts.

While Nixon's father Francis was a failed rancher and also began various small businesses that struggled, Kennedy's father Joseph P. Kennedy was a millionaire at a young age and had served as Ambassador to the Court of St. James during the presidency of Franklin Roosevelt. Nixon lost a brother to illness at a young age while Kennedy experienced the deaths of his oldest brother in the war and of his oldest sister soon after the war.

Kennedy's service in the House of Representatives was undistinguished while Nixon earned fame as part of the House Committee on Un-American Activities (HUAC) and as a key player in the search for Communists in the government. His anti-Communist credentials were established during his first campaign for Congress, and he generated considerable publicity when HUAC pursued State Department employee Alger Hiss as a suspected Communist.

That fame propelled him to the Senate where he again used his anti-Communist reputation to hint that the incumbent Senator Helen Gahagan Douglas was a Communist sympathizer. Kennedy didn't earn national attention until he was in the Senate and participated in Senate hearings seeking to rout out organized crime from the American labor movement.

In 1952, as Kennedy was seeking the Senate seat, Nixon was nominated to run for vice president on the Republican ticket with retired General Dwight D. Eisenhower, a truly national hero because of his leadership in the campaign to defeat Nazi Germany in the war. The Eisenhower-Nixon team was elected in 1952, and Nixon carved out a far more public role as vice president than the country had seen in the past.

He earned national attention while traveling in South America and standing up to riotous anti-American mobs and became more famous by debating Soviet leader Nikita Khrushchev at an American exhibition in Moscow, what became known as the *Kitchen Debate*.

On two occasions during the eight years of the Eisenhower presidency, Nixon was thrust into the role of "acting president" because of the president's heart attacks. He had every reason to consider himself a major player on the national stage, an accomplished anti-Communist, and a prominent leader of the Republican Party. When he won the Republican nomination to run for president in 1960, few Americans were surprised.

Kennedy also harbored national political ambition for many years. He first sought the Democratic nomination for vice president in 1956 when the Democratic presidential nominee Adlai Stevenson threw the matter open for the Democratic Convention to decide.

Narrowly losing that effort, he soon decided to mount a serious effort to win the presidential nomination in the 1960 election. Running what was easily the best-organized and best-funded campaign for the nomination ever, his victory at the Democratic Convention wasn't assured until the final votes were cast on the first ballot.

The stage was set. America would be going from the oldest president ever to one of the youngest, truly a new generation of leadership.

The post-convention polls reported a Nixon lead of 53–47% in one, and 50-44 in another. Of greater concern to Kennedy were polling details that said 31% of Nixon supporters were *very strongly* committed while only 22% of Kennedy supporters expressed the same level of intensity. The Kennedy camp found some comfort in the findings that 60% of Americans reported paying little or no attention to the presidential campaign so far.[cxxii]

There are always many factors that contribute to an election victory or defeat. Sometimes, world or national events like war, depression, or other crises can determine the election outcome despite the best efforts of either candidate. But there are other elections where a key decision made as part of the election strategy can make or break a campaign. Such was the story of Richard Nixon's narrow defeat in the 1960 presidential election.

There were two decisions made by Vice President Nixon that turned out badly and led to his election defeat. First, he announced that he would be the first presidential candidate to ever visit all 50 states. In fact, there never had been an election in which America had 50 states.

Alaska and Hawaii had been added to the Union the previous year. Traveling to each of these states was not easy in 1960 and polling had advanced to the point where it was becoming clear that Alaska would be a solid Republican state while Hawaii would be Democratic. That fact has remained consistent to this day.

The second decision, and one that had a huge impact on the campaign, was the Nixon agreement to debate Kennedy on national television.

President Eisenhower advised Nixon not to debate. He saw Nixon as far better known than Kennedy, and considered him more mature and experienced but, because he was clearly ahead in the race, should not give Kennedy the attention and audience he would receive by debating.[cxxiii]

The television networks, particularly NBC and CBS, lobbied Congress to make a temporary change in the equal time provision, currently in force. It would require all 16 candidates to be given the same access to the airwaves. The temporary suspension, eventually approved by Congress, would allow the networks to host debates between the two major candidates only.

Once the suspension passed, the debate challenge was presented to Nixon and Kennedy, and their campaign teams began negotiating the rules with the networks' representatives. The final agreement was for four debates: September 26, October 7, October 13, and October 21. The first would be produced at CBS in Chicago, the second by NBC in Washington, and the final two by ABC in New York.[cxxiv]

During the campaign, Nixon seriously banged his knee, which grew infected and sent him to the hospital. At that point, said Nixon advisor Pat Buchanan, he looked *sallow and gaunt* and should have decided not to go to all of the 50 states as promised. "It was a terrible mistake." On Nixon's pledge to visit all 50 states, former Sen. John Warner, who was then a Nixon campaign aide, said it was a bad formula, time spent for votes gained in order to go to Alaska and Hawaii. It *drained his energy*. Nixon's health and appearance, previously an advantage for the candidate, became a handicap instead.

Prof. Timothy Naftali said that Nixon traded away his physical advantage over the very sick JFK, which was being kept hidden by the Kennedy team.[cxxv] Kennedy had a bad back from his wartime injuries and suffered from Addison's disease, which was only revealed years later.

As the television debate neared, Nixon had barely recovered from his hospitalization but stubbornly continued his traveling to the two new states, further exhausting him.

The first debate would take place on September 26 and both campaigns negotiated its details with great care and urgency. All three networks would broadcast it live. There would be an eight-minute opening statement by each candidate and a three-minute closing statement. Nixon wanted no reaction shots but Kennedy's desire to include them prevailed.

Neither candidate would be shown wiping sweat from his face. While the networks wanted the candidates to question each other, neither candidate wanted that and it was agreed they would be questioned by a panel of reporters, one from each network.[cxxvi]

Doris Kearns Goodwin wrote a memoir about her life with Richard Goodwin, who was a Kennedy speech writer, and reminisced with her about the first debate. Goodwin told her that Kennedy was "Calm, almost eerily so" that morning. Despite the pressure he must have felt that day, Kennedy was able to nap in the afternoon after reviewing his stack of index cards that contained likely questions and suggested responses. Ted Sorensen, JFK's chief aide, Goodwin, and others were in and out of Kennedy's suite, often rushing around to find answers to the questions their candidate was raising that day.

Nixon, it was learned, spent the day in his hotel, secluded with only his wife Pat at his side.[cxxvii]

On CNN's 'Race for the White House: 1960 John F. Kennedy vs Richard Nixon', March-April 2016, Evan Thomas talked about Nixon watching Kennedy accept the Democratic Party's nomination on television. He considered the speech weak and thought JFK "came across as being privileged and effeminate; not good on TV."

He felt confident he could beat him. Nixon also underestimated the impact that the debates would have. No one really knew the role they would play at the time, being the first-ever televised national presidential debates. But Nixon felt confident that he'd do well. They generated the largest television audience up to that time, virtually 100% of the electorate watched.

In 1950, only 11% of America's 40 million households had TVs. By 1960, there were 10% more households than 10 years earlier but the number with TVs had risen to 88%.[cxxviii] An estimated 77 million people watched the first debate.

On the day of the debate, Nixon kept up his campaign schedule, even spending valuable time visiting the Carpenters' Union, which he knew would not endorse him. JFK, on the other hand, sunned himself on his hotel rooftop while being prepped by his staff.

When Nixon arrived at the TV studios, he was anxious, nervous and, unbelievably, banged his damaged knee on the car door when arriving. He was also in pain.

Naftali said that "Nixon arrived in agony."

When the two candidates were asked if they wanted make-up, Kennedy instantly replied that he did not. Nixon, needing to appear manly, agreed that he did not either. Kennedy proceeded to go backstage, and his staff applied make-up. Nixon stood around the stage asking questions about the format and making small talk. Kennedy returned to the stage just before the broadcast was to begin.

Buchanan said that, "Nixon made every mistake you could think of in that debate."

He constantly stated that he agreed with Kennedy and, while JFK was talking, the camera watched Nixon's eyes darting around, sweat beading on his face. His five o'clock shadow was evident, while Kennedy looked tanned, rested, and ready; presidential in fact. It has also been argued that Kennedy's

96

navy suit contrasted favorably with Nixon's light gray suit on black and white television.

Those who heard the debate on the radio judged Nixon the winner. However, the TV audience overwhelmingly tilted to Kennedy.

The GOP vice-presidential candidate, Henry Cabot Lodge, commented, "We've lost."

Evidence of that mounted in the days right after the first debate, as Kennedy's crowds swelled, and he was greeted like a conquering hero or a rock star.

Ironically, it was Lodge who had faced Kennedy in the 1952 Senatorial campaign and had experienced a similar result after observers had assumed the "debonair and experienced" Lodge should have prevailed over the youthful Jack Kennedy, which he did not.

Syndicated columnist and nationally known journalist Joseph Alsop commented after the debate, "Nixon looks like a suspect in a statutory rape case."[cxxix]

Theodore H. White wrote the first of his presidential campaign chronicles in 1960. He described in detail the contrasting appearances of the two candidates during the debates, making it clear that the television broadcasts served Kennedy more than Nixon.

He wrote, "When they began, Nixon was generally viewed as being the probable winner of the election contest and Kennedy as fighting an uphill battle; when they were over, the positions of the two contestants were reversed." He went on to describe the "quantum jump in the size of crowds that greeted" Kennedy beginning the morning after the first debate.[cxxx]

By the time all four debates had concluded, the Gallup poll wrote that 85 million Americans had watched at least one of the debates. The surveys by the networks claimed an even larger audience with NBC's estimate at 115 million and CBS setting the number at 120 million. The CBS survey also reported that 57% of the country felt their votes were influenced by the debates.[cxxxi]

The result was the closest election in the century with the highest turnout to date. More than 68 million votes were cast, and Kennedy squeaked by with a margin of .17%, about 112,000 votes.

Kennedy intimates Kenneth O'Donnell and Dave Powers wrote in a biography of their late friend that "The contrast on the television screen between Nixon's nervous anxiety and Kennedy's cool composure wiped away the Republican contention that Kennedy was too immature and inexperienced for the Presidency and established him as a potential winner. It also brought several more reluctant Democratic notables scurrying to get under Kennedy's umbrella."[cxxxii]

Arthur Krock, then the Washington bureau chief for the *New York Times* and a renowned political columnist, wrote, "I share the view that when Nixon agreed to the TV debates with Kennedy, on the terms both accepted, he took an unnecessary gamble that cost him hundreds of thousands of votes in an election that was decided by a popular plurality of 118,574 [sic] in a total of 68,838,219 votes cast."[cxxxiii]

Historian Merrill Peterson wrote that "Kennedy owed his narrow victory over Nixon in 1960, in part, to the public verdict for him in the celebrated television debates that recalled the Lincoln-Douglas debates but, everyone agreed, scarcely compared with them."[cxxxiv]

In Doris Kearns Goodwin's memoir, she describes the aftermath of the first debate by writing, "The more striking impression on television, however, belonged to Kennedy. He seemed to ignore Nixon altogether, making his case directly to the people on the other side of the camera: Watching the two men side by side, the contention that Vice President Nixon was the more seasoned and mature candidate, possessed of greater authority and capacity to lead, had vanished before the first debate was over."

She goes on to add, "something decisive and positive had happened for Kennedy during the debate, something that could be seen, felt, and heard in Ohio the next morning. The crowds hadn't merely doubled, they had quadrupled, as had the intensity, excitement, energy, and high-pitched screams. Those millions of television sets that had been tuned in to the debate the night before had given birth to a political celebrity of the first order."[cxxxv]

Nixon didn't need to do this. There was no precedent; no presidential debates on TV before 1960. In fact, previous efforts to get Presidents Franklin Roosevelt and Dwight Eisenhower to debate on the radio during their campaigns came to naught.[cxxxvi] Nixon was ahead in the polls and could have safely avoided the TV confrontation.

He saw himself as a serious candidate and Kennedy as a spoiled rich kid, a dilettante who didn't know the issues as the vice president did. The debates can be described as a serious miscalculation by Nixon in the way he judged his opponent.

Richard Nixon wrote about the debates in his memoirs. He stated that he knew the debates would benefit Kennedy more than himself. But he adds that refusing to debate would have created an issue for Kennedy and the media that would have damaged his campaign. Nixon also felt that foreign policy was his greatest strength as an issue and wanted the first debate to focus on that.

But his advisors argued that the TV audience would grow, and he would be better off in having the fourth debate about foreign policy. He regretted conceding to his advisors and allowing domestic policy to be the subject of the first debate.

He also wrote, "It is a devastating commentary on the nature of television as a political medium that what hurt me the most in the first debate was not the substance of the encounter between Kennedy and me, but the disadvantageous contrast in our physical appearances. After the program ended, callers, including my mother, wanted to know if anything was wrong, because I did not look well."[cxxxvii]

John Kennedy fully expected to one day write his memoirs and discussed that prospect with his closest advisor, Ted Sorensen. Given the intimacy of the two men over a period of 11 years, having Sorensen's account of the debate is the next best thing.

He wrote that Kennedy reacted quickly to the offer to debate from the networks, hoping there could be five or more debates, and bluntly issued a challenge to Nixon. "The four debates, and the first in particular, played a decisive role in the election results. Nixon knew it. Kennedy knew it. Their advisors and party leaders knew it. The crowds reflected it." He adds that 25% of voters in August who had not expected to vote changed their minds and voted in November, with most of them voting for Kennedy. "More than four out of five voters saw or heard at least one of the four debates, the average adult saw three, and more than half of all adults watched all four." The debates helped Kennedy solidify his Democratic support and win over independents by more than two to one.[cxxxviii]

Kennedy's experience with the debate led him to consider a series of debates with the likely, and eventual, Republican presidential nominee Barry Goldwater when they would be facing off in 1964. Kennedy's assassination in 1963 made that plan impossible and his successor, Lyndon Johnson, probably never even considered debating Goldwater prior to crushing him in the 1964 election.

Nixon had learned his lesson and refused to debate the Democratic nominee, Vice President Hubert Humphrey, when they faced off in 1968. Humphrey labeled Nixon "Sir-Richard-the-Chicken-Hearted."[cxxxix] In fact, there were no televised presidential debates for 16 years after the Nixon-Kennedy debate.

Once they started up again in 1976, they have become regular events every four years and often play a major role in the election outcome, though not always. Jimmy Carter and President Gerald Ford debated in 1976, and the debates had a huge impact on the outcome. Four years later, in 1980, President Jimmy Carter and Republican nominee Ronald Reagan prepared to face off in televised debates.

Nixon, then in exile six years after resigning from the presidency, discussed the upcoming debate with the Reagan campaign. "I wish I could give you a lot of advice, based on my experience of winning political debates. But I don't have that experience. My only experience is at losing them."[cxl]

Had Nixon avoided the travel to Alaska and Hawaii, he would have been in better physical shape for the first TV debate. Had he debated only on radio or not at all, it's easy to argue that he would have won the presidency in 1960. From his standpoint, agreeing to debate John Kennedy on television was a bad decision.

Lyndon B. Johnson – Courtesy of the LBJ Presidential Library

Lyndon Johnson – Quagmire

One of the many books written about Lyndon Baines Johnson after his presidency was called *The Tragedy of Lyndon Johnson* by one of his White House Counselors, Eric Goldman. This is an incredibly appropriate title because there are many ways to discuss the presidency that should have been and the tragedy it became.

Former U.S. Senator Birch Bayh described LBJ by saying, "He would have been considered one of the great ones if it hadn't been for Vietnam."

Elder statesman Averell Harriman said, "LBJ was great in domestic affairs. Harry Truman had programs, but none got through. Kennedy had no technique. FDR talked simply during the crisis but didn't act enough later. Johnson went back past the New Frontier all the way to the New Deal. He loved FDR, and it was fantastic what he did. If it hadn't been for…Vietnam he'd have been the greatest president ever. Even so, he'll still be remembered as great."[cxli]

One reviewer of Goldman's book wrote that "Goldman's Johnson is intelligent, manipulative, overbearing, cornball, thin-skinned, mistrustful, secretive, vain, devious, dishonest, competitive, and something of an idealist."[cxlii]

LBJ was, in short, a very interesting character.

The life of Lyndon Johnson has been well-chronicled. Robert Caro and Robert Dallek wrote notable works as did Doris Kearns Goodwin. Her book was published shortly after she married Richard Goodwin but had not yet taken his name. It is fascinating as a first-person biography, written from her personal experiences with the late president.

There were so many successes and accomplishments in the political history of Lyndon Johnson. Born in 1908 and raised in the hardscrabble life of Johnson City, Texas along the Pedernales River, he rose to the highest heights in his chosen world of politics. He worked as a high school teacher and saw first-hand what it was like to be poor and Hispanic in rural America.

From there, he became a Congressional assistant and soon became one of the best-known staff members in the House of Representatives and a force in the Congressional district in which he served. Elected speaker of the "Little Congress," a group of Congressional staffers, he cultivated relations with leaders in Congress and the Franklin Delano Roosevelt White House.

In 1935, as part of FDR's New Deal, Johnson was appointed to be head of the Texas National Youth Administration, where he created job opportunities for a score of young people. In 1937, he won a special election for the House of Representatives, where he served until 1949.

As a member of Congress, LBJ took over the leadership of the moribund Democratic Congressional Campaign Committee (DCCC) and turned it into a major player in tight Congressional elections, endearing him to those colleagues who were indebted to him for their election successes. When World War II broke out, he joined the Navy, where he served honorably.

Three years after the war ended, he was elected to the U.S. Senate, where he served from 1949 until he became vice president, elected on the Democratic ticket with John F. Kennedy in 1960.

There has been lots of speculation as to why JFK chose Johnson to be his running mate. What seems obvious now was that he needed Johnson's help in winning the electoral votes of Texas, but more importantly, knew that he would be dependent on LBJ if Johnson remained majority leader in the Senate. During the previous presidency, that of Dwight D. Eisenhower, LBJ was the most dominant and effective majority leader the Senate had ever seen.

He ruled his Democratic majority in a manner that was never matched before or since. Never an ally of JFK while serving together in the Senate, an alliance between the new president and LBJ would have been difficult at best. One reason that they had never been allies was LBJ's opinion of his junior colleague.

Kennedy's record of accomplishment in the Senate was meager while Johnson's was substantial, something that led LBJ to view Kennedy in a patronizing manner. And they both sought the Democratic presidential nomination in 1960 with Kennedy prevailing. The previously dominant Johnson was soon to play second fiddle to a man LBJ considered too young, too inexperienced, too unsubstantial.

Johnson was substantial. His record in Congress was where he first made his mark. He was instrumental in bringing electricity to the rural areas of his Congressional district.

As a senator, he was the major force in helping pass the key foreign and domestic accomplishments of the Eisenhower presidency: the National Aeronautics and Space Act, creating NASA, the Federal-Aid Highway Act of 1956, establishing the interstate highway system, and, in the area of civil rights, led the Senate to pass the Civil Rights Acts of 1957 and 1960.

The latter are notable because Johnson represented a southern state and southern senators had been a significant obstacle to passing civil rights measures for decades, but he prevailed. Johnson's mastery of his Senate leadership was unmatched, and he took pride in his accomplishments.

But now, Johnson was to be vice president. He accepted the offer from Kennedy knowing he would no longer be the country's top Democrat and felt it was his duty to not only support Kennedy's election but to defeat the Republican nominee, Richard Nixon. He also realized that his role as Senate majority leader in a Democratic administration would be vastly different than it had been under Eisenhower.

If he turned down the vice-presidential offer and remained in the Senate, he would not be the number one Democrat in the country any longer as he had been, should Kennedy be elected. What Johnson could not have known was the role he would end up playing in a Kennedy administration.

The relationship between Kennedy's brother Robert, the campaign manager and JFK's choice to be attorney general, is well-chronicled. The enmity between the two was substantial and Robert Kennedy never tried to conceal his distaste of LBJ, nor his negative views about his brother's choice for the vice presidency.

While LBJ would later talk about the courtesies he regularly received from President Kennedy, he bristled because of the secondary role he was given in the administration. Largely confined to ceremonial duties and ignored in those meetings in which he took part, Johnson was about as unhappy in the vice presidency as any of his predecessors had been.

All of that changed on November 22, 1963. John F. Kennedy was assassinated in Dallas, Texas and Lyndon Baines Johnson became the 36th president of the United States.

LBJ was probably as prepared to be president as any man before him had been. He knew the office intimately as a creature of Congress as well as the vice president. And he had served as a master of the Senate. He quickly showed the country that he was in charge, respectfully promoting the unfinished business of the martyred President Kennedy.

Within a year of the assassination, he had successfully steered to passage the Civil Rights Act of 1964, the most far-reaching measure for civil rights that the country had ever witnessed. He was elected in his own right in 1964, in one of the greatest presidential landslides ever, receiving the highest percentage of popular votes than any president since James Monroe.

The next year he was successful in passing the Voting Rights Act, further cementing his reputation as the greatest civil rights president and prominent legislative leader. LBJ knew he had a mandate and intended to use it. The Great Society was announced by Johnson in 1964 and presented to Congress early in 1965, a series of domestic programs aimed at eliminating poverty, ending racial injustice, and creating greater opportunities for every child in America.

The goals of LBJ's Great Society and his war on poverty were monumental and sought to change the country in many ways. He promoted massive spending programs seeking to provide equal education for all, universal medical care, an end to poverty, urban renewal, and great improvement in public transportation. With FDR as his model, he sought to outdo what the New Deal had done for the country and earn a spot for himself as the greatest president ever.

"The Great Society would offer something to almost everyone: Medicare for the old, educational assistance for the young, tax rebates for business, a higher minimum wage for labor, subsidies for farmers, vocational training for the unskilled, food for the hungry, housing for the homeless, poverty grants for the poor, clean highways for commuters, legal protection for the blacks, improved schooling for the Indians, rehabilitation for the lame, higher benefits for the unemployed, reduced quotas for the immigrants, auto safety for drivers, pensions for the retired, fair labeling for consumers, conservation for the hikers and the campers, and more and more and more. None of his fellow citizens' desires were, Johnson thought, wholly beyond his ability to satisfy."[cxliii]

Vietnam, moreover, was a blip on the radar screen when LBJ was re-elected. Only 30% of the public in 1964 felt that it was the country's most urgent problem.[cxliv]

All presidents, however, have to balance the interests of foreign and domestic policy and seek to wisely divide public spending between what has been known as *guns and butter*. But LBJ wanted both – his Great Society and victory in Vietnam. While LBJ was seeking his Great Society in 1965–1966, he was also escalating the American role in Vietnam.

By that time, the number of Americans feeling that Vietnam was the country's most urgent issue rose to 60%, double what it was at the time of the re-election. Nonetheless, Johnson still enjoyed a 64% approval rating and was considered the most admired American in the world, with Eisenhower in second place and Robert Kennedy third. Three-fourths of the country approved LBJ's handling of the Vietnam conflict and tilted strongly against anti-war protestors.[cxlv]

When the United States began its involvement in the conflict in Vietnam, few Americans even knew where it was. Vietnam had been a long-time French colony until shortly after World War II. French control of that area of southeast Asia continued until 1954, when they were thrown out by Vietnamese guerilla armies.

After that, a Geneva Conference partitioned Vietnam into two countries, Communist North Vietnam, and the State of Vietnam, later the Republic of Vietnam, in the south. It was supposed to be a temporary partition until elections could be held.

Ho Chi Minh, the leader of the Communist north, was a revolutionary and nationalist who sought to unite the country. Had he not declared himself to be a Communist, the western democracies might have cared less about his efforts. However, the civil war that Ho led was viewed by the anti-Communist British and American leaders as Communist aggression.

The history of British appeasement that led to World War II was fresh in the memories of these leaders, who felt that the Communists needed to be stopped wherever they were trying to advance. A prominent theory at the time was called the Domino Theory. It concluded that letting one country fall to the Communists would lead to others falling soon after, eventually threatening our own shores.

American involvement in French-Indochina began with the Truman administration, providing aid to the French in their efforts to control the region and stop the Communist advances. When the French left, the Eisenhower administration provided aid to the government in Vietnam's south. The planned election would not be held with President Eisenhower concerned that Ho Chi Minh might win.

It was felt that the only acceptable way for the country to be united was to make the Republic of Vietnam successful and to help it oust the Communists in the north. That policy continued into the Kennedy administration as increasing aid was provided and American advisors were sent to South Vietnam.

When LBJ became president, he felt trapped. To leave the South Vietnamese and see the country go Communist was reminiscent of the experience when we *lost China*, the era when the Chinese Communists took over that nation. The reaction in the United States was the birth of McCarthyism, as anti-Communism grew in popularity.

LBJ didn't want to be remembered as the president who lost Vietnam to the Communists. He knew that fully supporting the South Vietnamese would threaten his domestic programs, but he persisted in trying to have it both ways. He felt he couldn't, in his own words, *cut and run*.

Many scholars have debated what the future of the Kennedy administration would have meant to Vietnam. In interviews just prior to his assassination, Kennedy had said that in the final analysis, it was South Vietnam's war to win or lose.

It has been speculated that JFK would have left Vietnam after being re-elected against Senator Barry Goldwater, that leaving earlier would have only helped the Goldwater campaign. But we will never know for sure. His successor, Lyndon Johnson, retained Kennedy's advisors and they encouraged him to support South Vietnam.

LBJ's closest colleague in the Senate, Richard Russell of Georgia, was opposed to American intervention in the war and urged Johnson to get out. Russell had not just been an esteemed colleague but was almost a father figure to LBJ and his wife Lady Bird. As our intervention increased, other leaders began to express their opposition to American involvement.

And as our involvement grew, American casualties did as well. Having American advisors in Vietnam was one thing but Johnson pivoted to troops on the ground. And as those troop levels proved unable to accomplish American goals, the troop levels were increased. As increasing numbers of Americans were being killed in Vietnam, opposition to the war grew.

Americans' first TV war, the nightly news broadcasts featured body bags carrying killed American boys. As Johnson feared, the opposition to Vietnam threatened his domestic priorities as well.

Johnson experienced a myriad of conflicting thoughts about his dilemma. The United States had won World War II, was the strongest nation on the planet, and the idea that a measly country called Vietnam could defeat it was preposterous. What had America ever tried to do that it could not? But what would the cost be to win the war?

Putting aside the number of casualties that it might mean, would an American victory only bring in the other Communist adversaries, particularly China and the Soviet Union? That could mean World War III. He hoped he could provide enough pressure on North Vietnam to bring them to the table and negotiate a settlement. The LBJ treatment that was so successful with senators could be equally successful with Ho Chi Minh.

Rather than see Ho as a freedom fighter who only cared about uniting his country, he saw him as a bully trying to impose his will on those in the south who wanted to fight Communism.

LBJ had been quoted as saying, "Whether communist or fascist or simply a pistol-packing racketeer, the one thing a bully understands is force and the one thing he fears is courage…I want peace. But human experience teaches me that if I let a bully of my community make me travel the back streets to avoid a fight, I merely postpone the evil day. Soon he will chase me out of my house… If you let a bully come into your front yard, the next day he'll be up on your porch, and the day after that he'll rape your wife in your own bed. But if you say to him at the start, 'Now, just hold on, wait a minute', then he'll know he's dealing with a man of courage, someone who will stand up to him. And only then can you get along and find some peace again."[cxlvi]

He worried that efforts to make peace might also make him look weak. But he also worried that being too aggressive and destructive to North Vietnam might bring on a bigger war. He found himself in a policy dilemma, unlike anything he had experienced domestically when he never entered a battle in which he couldn't foresee the end game.

He entered this battle with little understanding of how it might end but envisioned how he might help heal the Vietnamese after it ended, however that might be.

In retirement, he rambled to Doris Kearns about how he couldn't "let Ho Chi Minh run through the streets of Saigon," comparing such an approach as similar to Neville Chamberlain appeasing Hitler prior to World War II. He saw the loss of China to the Communists during the Truman presidency as causing the rise of McCarthyism.

He went on to say, "there would be Robert Kennedy out in front leading the fight against me, telling everyone that I had betrayed John Kennedy's commitment to South Vietnam. That I had let a democracy fall into the hands of the communists. That I was a coward. An unmanly man. A man without a spine. Oh, I could see it coming all right. Every night, when I fell asleep I would see myself tied to the ground in the middle of a long, open space. In the distance, I could hear the voices of thousands of people. They were all shouting at me and running toward me: 'Coward! Traitor! Weakling!'"

That weakness he described would be exploited by Russia and China and the country would be blackmailed because of him.

"I was bound to be crucified either way I moved."[cxlvii]

When discussing civil rights with a senator, who described the civil rights battles as a dilemma, "Johnson said he faced dilemmas *all day here, all day long*," including a recent decision about whether to send two battalions of marines to South Vietnam to protect an American air base near Danang.

Johnson feared he was stepping deeper into a morass, one that might sink his ambitious domestic agenda. Stress over Vietnam disturbed Johnson's sleep and corroded his personality, leaving him depressed, making his family's life *pure hell*, as Lady Bird Johnson put it.[cxlviii]

But American patience was being tested as never before as millions of Americans began marching in the streets to protest the war.

It's not difficult to understand LBJ's frustration. He felt he had done so much for those in the country who needed help the most but there was rioting in the streets by many of those same people. He had a hard time understanding why so many young Americans were protesting against their own country at war.

And the politicians he had ruled over for so many years were also seemingly in revolt. George Reedy, who had been a White House press secretary for part of the Johnson administration, wrote a book about the presidency a few years after the end of that administration. It was called *The Twilight of the Presidency* and described the problems facing Johnson in this manner. "The troubles of our country are painfully apparent. The war in Vietnam still chews up our youth. Our college students are on rampages without precedent in our history. Inflation is bringing millions of Americans close to the edge of economic hardship. Negro militants are challenging not only their past inferiority in a segregated society but the validity of the liberal dream of a fully integrated society."[cxlix]

When LBJ spoke about his aspirations, about the kind of president he wanted to be, about the battle for civil rights and the Great Society, he said, "I do not want to be the President who built empires, or sought grandeur, or extended dominion. I want to be the President who educated young children…who helped to feed the hungry…who helped the poor to find their own way and who protected the right of every citizen to vote in every election…God will not favor everything we do. It is rather our duty to divine His will. But I cannot help believing that He truly understands and that He really favors the undertaking that we begin tonight."

Doris Kearns reflected on those words and saw that he was a true believer, just as he was about Vietnam. But she added, on these issues and not Vietnam, he had a "far more lucid sense of the human and political realities."[cl]

Johnson had become a close ally of the Reverend Martin Luther King, Jr. during the effort to pass the Civil Rights Act of 1964 and the Voting Rights Act of 1965. But even King weighed in with concerns about Vietnam in a phone call in 1965.

"King got the impression that Johnson knew he had *made a mistake in Vietnam but does not know how to get out of it.*" King's outspokenness on Vietnam created a gap between the two men that was never repaired.[cli] As he feared, LBJ's focus on Vietnam would diminish his attention on civil rights and would end up reducing the funding available for the domestic agenda.

As he raised his public profile against the war, King saw that he *may have contributed to a shift in white liberal activism*, away from civil rights and more toward ending the war.[clii] On March 16, 1968, King announced that he would not support President Johnson's re-election. Telling reporters how proud he was of the work he had done with the president on the landmark civil rights legislation; "it all came down to Vietnam now, King said."[cliii]

By late 1967, LBJ was seeing his own political future under threat. First, Sen. Eugene McCarthy of Minnesota entered the primaries against him, followed soon by a greater threat, New York Sen. Robert Kennedy, his long-time antagonist.

As McCarthy nearly defeated Johnson in the nation's first primary in New Hampshire, Kennedy entered the fray, and Lyndon Johnson threw in the towel. The nation was stunned when a televised speech about Vietnam turned into a Johnson announcement that he was not a candidate for re-election.

Doris Kearns wrote that it was "impossible for Johnson to understand the tumult in the streets, the continuing capacity of the North Vietnamese to resist his will, or his own steadily deteriorating popularity. After all, he believed, he had given more laws, more houses, more medical services, more loans, and more promises to more people than any President in history. Surely, he had earned the love and gratitude of the American people. Yet as he looked around him in 1967 and 1968 he saw only paralyzing bitterness and hatred. Uncomprehending and deeply hurt as he was, it was natural that he would seek the cause of his decline in the personal animosity and motives of individual enemies – the press, the Eastern intellectuals, and the Kennedys – and even more natural, though surprising at first glance, that he would decide to withdraw from the world of politics and go back to the place where he was born, where, at least, as his father had told him years before, 'The people know when you're sick and care when you die'."[cliv]

Johnson, in 1970, told Kearns, "I knew from the start that I was bound to be crucified either way I moved. If I left the woman I really loved – the Great Society – in order to get involved with that bitch of a war on the other side of the world, then I would lose everything at home. All my programs. All my hopes to feed the hungry and shelter the homeless. All my dreams to provide education and medical care to the browns and the blacks and the lame and the poor. But if I left that war and let the Communists take over South Vietnam, then I would be seen as a coward and my nation would be seen as an appeaser and we would both find it impossible to accomplish anything for anybody anywhere on the entire globe."[clv]

Doris Kearns Goodwin, long after her marriage to Richard Goodwin and after his death, wrote a memoir in which she reflected more about those conversations with LBJ.

Few leaders in history had craved attention more than Lyndon Johnson had and few had been, for months on end, more savagely jeered and derided.

By the end of March, the president's approval rating had dropped to 36 percent, the lowest of his career. The percentage of those supporting his handling of the war had fallen to 26 percent. He had lost the people's trust.

The administration's optimistic projections about the progress of the war collided with the reality reported in newspapers and magazines. In the weeks after the Tet Offensive, seven major newspapers, including *The Wall Street Journal*, the *New York Post*, and the *St. Louis Post-Dispatch* had turned against the war.

"I felt that I was being chased on all sides by a giant stampede coming at me from all directions," Johnson later told me, speaking of that late winter and early spring of 1968.

On one side the American people were stampeding me to do something about Vietnam. On another side, the inflationary economy [the result of Johnson's earlier refusal to call for a war tax] was booming out of control. Up ahead were dozens of danger signs pointing to another summer of riots in the cities. I was being forced over the edge by rioting blacks and demonstrating students.

The man who had basked in the affection of crowds could no longer venture into major cities without encountering protestors chanting:
"Hey, Hey, LBJ, how many kids did you kill today?" No longer finding pleasure in daily activities, he dreaded the nights of insomnia even more. When able to fitfully sleep, he was beset by a recurring anxiety dream. As he recounted it to me later, *he saw himself swimming in a river. He was swimming from the center toward one shore. He swam and swam but never seemed to get any closer. He turned around to swim to the other shore, but again he got nowhere. He was simply going round and round in circles.*[clvi]

Johnson could always see an end game in domestic politics. He felt sure-footed and competent. In foreign policy, however, he was less sure of himself and depended much more on the advice of others. With Vietnam, seeing the end game was more difficult and LBJ pursued his policy without really having a formulated result. Embarking on a policy he supported, the build-up became inexorable.

American troop strength in Vietnam at the time of the Kennedy-Johnson election was only 800. By the end of LBJ's first full year as president, it had risen to 23,000 and, a year later, to 184,000. By 1967, the numbers had risen to half a million. Casualties rose in a similar fashion. The killed, wounded, hospitalized, and missing were 2,500 in 1965, 33,000 in 1966, 80,000 in 1967, and 130,000 in 1968.[clvii]

With 525,000 American troops in Vietnam in 1967 and more than 12,000 killed and 75,000 wounded, the country was spending about $2 billion a month on the war.

"And yet, in the opinion of most disinterested observers, the war is not going well. Victory is not close at hand. It is clearly unlikely in the next year or even the next two years. American officers talk somberly about fighting here for decades," reported *The New York Times* from Vietnam that summer.[clviii]

While he depended so much more on the advice of others in foreign policy, his advisors recommended a different course on Vietnam than he chose to pursue. He was advised to *go to the Congress, declare a state of emergency, and put the economy on a wartime footing*. Johnson refused and chose instead to hide the costs of the war from the American people, *keeping the pretense of a peacetime economy*. Should he come clean with the American public, he was sure his Great Society would go down in flames.

Kearns describes the environment inside the White House clearly and adds, "As it turns out, however, the people were not hurt by knowing too much; Lyndon Johnson was hurt by knowing too little."

"The loss of public debate on the war lessened the possibilities of judgment, depriving Johnson of the chance to test various responses to different policies and of the opportunity to dispel misconceptions. Nor, in the absence of any clear understanding of the goals in Vietnam, could he expect to sustain the public's support."[clix]

The reality of the modern presidency is its domination of the public's attention. And Lyndon Johnson, the man who had dominated the Senate when serving as its leader, similarly dominated American politics during his presidency. The Great Society became his program. Vietnam, therefore, became his war. He, "personally, was dropping the bombs, disrupting the economy, making prices rise, setting back the progress of black and poor."[clx]

His decisions to pursue the American intervention in Vietnam, based on inaccurate assumptions, destroyed his legacy and cost thousands of lives. He had assumed he could pursue his domestic dreams while expanding the American role in the war. He assumed that he was pursuing a policy set by his predecessor.

He assumed that his legacy upon leaving Vietnam would be one of a coward and an undependable ally. He assumed that if he was candid with the country about the real expenses of his Vietnam policy, he would lose support for his Great Society.

So, he determined to hide those costs, resulting in a generation of Americans who felt they could no longer trust what their government told them. And he assumed that the American people would see how he was improving their lives and tolerate his war-making in southeast Asia.

As Doris Kearns wrote in her book about LBJ, "Lyndon Johnson had wanted to surpass Franklin Roosevelt; and Roosevelt, after all, had not only won the reforms Johnson envied, he had also waged a war. But there was a critical difference: Roosevelt did not attempt the New Deal and World War II at the same time. Only Johnson among the Presidents sought to be simultaneously first in peace and first in war; and even Johnson was bound to fail."[clxi]

Johnson's decision to use American might to force a victory by the non-Communist forces in Vietnam cost him and the nation dearly. It ruined LBJ's legacy and forced him from office. In many ways, it changed American opinion about their own nation. And it cost hundreds of thousands of Americans their lives.

The number of Vietnamese killed by the American escalation of the war is incalculable. The repercussions from Johnson's decisions have affected the United States ever since.

Richard M. Nixon – Courtesy the Library of Congress

Richard Nixon – Burn the Tapes

Richard Nixon is a fascinating historical figure. He dominated much of American politics for a quarter of a century and was involved in a number of major events requiring many significant decisions. As a member of the House of Representatives in the post-war period of the late 1940s, he became famous as an anti-Communist investigator, enmeshed in the Alger Hiss controversy.

His fame led him to a successful campaign for the U.S. Senate from California and, in 1952, onto the Republican ticket for vice president, running with Dwight Eisenhower.

The Eisenhower/Nixon campaign was successful but only after Nixon had to decide how best to deal with a controversy concerning a slush fund that was formed to help him cover personal expenses. He decided to face the nation on television, giving what has become known as the *Checkers Speech*.

As maudlin as it may seem today, in 1952 it was a rousing success for the Republicans, allowing Nixon to remain on the ticket and become vice president. His decision to confront the issue on a national broadcast turned out to be a good one.

He made similar decisions while vice president, one in particular greatly enhanced his public image. When Soviet Premier Nikita Khrushchev toured the United States in 1959, he was looking over a display of modern American inventions used in a typical kitchen. Debating the nature of American innovations that made lives easier for the average American, what became known as the *Kitchen Debate* between the two men, showed the vice president successfully taking on the Communist leader while standing up for the United States and the American way of life.

After two terms as vice president, Nixon became the Republican nominee for the presidency. As chronicled here in another chapter, a decision he made to challenge the Democratic nominee, John F. Kennedy, to a televised debate was a bad decision that largely decided the election for Kennedy.

After the election loss, Nixon made another decision that didn't turn out so well. He decided to run for governor of California in 1962 and was handed another election defeat. When the election results were known, Nixon made a sour-grapes speech to the press, lambasting them for what he felt had been unfair coverage, telling them it was his last press conference, that they *"won't have Dick Nixon to kick around anymore."* It wouldn't have been unusual to consider him done with national politics, an unsuccessful political figure who would fade away into private life.

Not so. After thriving in a legal practice in New York, he began speaking out on public issues once again. As the incumbent President Lyndon Johnson's unpopularity grew over the Vietnam War and unrest in American cities, racial issues as well as the war, Nixon's profile kept rising. Soon, he was considered a viable candidate for the Republican presidential nomination in 1968.

Nixon would go on to win the nomination and, because President Johnson declined to run for re-election, the campaign would be against Vice President Hubert Humphrey. This time, there would be no challenge to a televised debate, at least not by Nixon. Humphrey issued the challenge this time and Nixon declined. He ran his campaign as "The New Nixon" with a secret plan to end the war in Vietnam.

The Democrats nominated Humphrey at a raucous, disruptive convention and despite the problems facing the incumbent party, the election ended up incredibly close, decided by less than 1% of the popular vote.

However, another Nixon decision made during the campaign could have brought disaster to his electoral chances. Worried that President Johnson would find a way to end the Vietnam War before the election, ensuring a victory for Humphrey, Nixon negotiated with the enemy, the North Vietnamese, in an illegal, some say traitorous, manner.

The message the Vietnamese received was that waiting for a Nixon election would be better for them than negotiating with the Johnson administration. It turns out that FBI wiretaps revealed the scheme to Johnson but making the issue public would have revealed the existence of the wiretaps. Johnson demurred and Nixon got away with behavior that clearly violated American law. He dodged a bullet and became president.

As president, Nixon made a number of policy decisions that had a major impact on American politics as well as history. His opening up of China with his administration talking directly to the Communist Chinese leadership after decades of silence was a major breakthrough that increased Nixon's popularity.

Similarly, his direct negotiations with the Soviet Union showed President Nixon to be a peacemaker like Americans had never known. These events cemented his role as an international leader and virtually guaranteed his re-election in 1972.

He was the ideal American leader to have taken these actions. As a strident anti-Communist for decades, his approach toward making peace with his Communist adversaries was seen as statesmanlike rather than political. He not only opened a dialogue with the People's Republic of China but traveled there himself in 1972.

And if that wasn't enough, he directed negotiations with the Soviet Union toward improving relations and traveled there as well during that tumultuous year. Both visits generated substantial national press coverage and Nixon's re-election prospects were secure. They even became more certain as South Dakota Senator George McGovern, probably his weakest Democratic opponent, secured the presidential nomination of his Party.

In Nixon's memoirs, he recounted how strong he was as he faced the 1972 election.

I do not believe that any administration in history has gone into a re-election campaign with a more impressive record than ours in August 1972. There was no major area of American life in which we had not made progress or proposed dramatic new alternatives.

He went on to describe how the inflation of 6.1% in 1969 had been cut to 2.7% in 1972. The stock market was moving toward record highs and the real earnings of Americans had been stagnant from 1965 to 1970 but were moving up at an annual rate of 4% by the election year. Farm income was higher, federal income taxes had been lowered, and major welfare reform had been proposed.

The Nixon administration had made major proposals on health insurance reform, toward reducing illegal drug use, and the previous rise in serious crime had been greatly reduced. There were educational initiatives, environmental gains, increased spending for the arts, and social security benefits had been increased. The military draft calls in 1968 rose to nearly 300,000 and were reduced to 50,000 in 1972, while the administration was moving toward an all-volunteer army with the draft eliminated.[clxii]

The desire to be re-elected burned strongly with Richard Nixon and he made a series of decisions designed to help his re-election that ended up leading to his demise. And, because of his strong political stature at the time, these decisions were totally unnecessary.

Several of the acts that were taken by members of his administration were probably not a result of a direct order of the president or even something he knew about. But a mentality seemed to envelop the White House, one of paranoia about perceived enemies and an insecurity about the political future.

Having lost two major elections in his life, that insecurity may be understandable, but Richard Nixon became enmeshed in the growing scandal that grew within this mindset.

The result became what will always be known as the Watergate scandal. Various illegalities had taken place by Nixon operatives aimed at tarnishing his political opponents. But it all began to unravel after the break-in at the Democratic National Committee in the Watergate apartment/hotel complex. Nixon and his top aides conspired to cover up the crimes.

In his memoirs, Nixon reflects on those actions that sealed his fate: "It was in these days at the end of June and the beginning of July 1972 that I took the first steps down the road that eventually led to the end of my presidency. I did nothing to discourage the various stories that were being considered to explain the break-in, and I approved efforts to encourage the CIA to intervene and limit the FBI investigation. Later, my actions and inactions during this period would appear to many as part of a widespread and conscious cover-up. I did not see them as such. I was handling in a pragmatic way what I perceived as an annoying and strictly political problem. I was looking for a way to deal with Watergate that would minimize the damage to me, my friends, and my campaign, while giving the least advantage to my political opponents. I saw Watergate as politics pure and simple. We were going to play it tough. I never doubted that that was exactly how the other side would have played it."[clxiii]

The Watergate scandal would eventually lead to the resignation of President Richard Nixon, the only such event in American history. However, it can be argued that many of the events falling under the Watergate rubric weren't direct decisions by the president but more the result of this mentality existing within his administration.

Instances of illegal wiretapping of people on his "enemies list" as well as illegal break-ins, particularly of the Democratic headquarters at the Watergate, may not have been decisions Nixon made himself but the effort to cover them up was largely orchestrated by him.

Understanding this mentality within the administration as well as Nixon's own psychology has been the object of study since Nixon's presidency. The author Fawn Brodie wrote a book examining the character of Nixon. She described him as a *man of paradox* who "promised to bring us truth in government, and instead brought us massive untruth…the Quaker president who ordered more bombs dropped than any man in history…He had the ambition to win more electoral votes than any president save Washington…but could still say to John Dean early in 1973, 'Nobody is a friend of ours; let's face it'….He is the supreme anti-Communist, who nevertheless establishes friendly relations with the largest bloc of Communists on the globe…He professes to have no interest in wealth but shows an exaggerated fondness for the trappings and pageantry of royalty, including fancy-dress uniforms for the White House guards and plans for the most palatial of presidential yachts. He is a man of extraordinary fastidiousness in dress whose language in private is foul…He is uptight with people…and has severe problems with intimacy and loving, yet is capable of pouring out his feelings in print…He can say on the one hand, 'Without enemies, my life would be dull as hell', yet complain shrilly of abuse by his political opponents and the press."[clxiv]

Brodie also writes about the paranoia referred to above, quoting White House aide Charles Colson. "Everybody thinks the people surrounding the President were drunk with power, but it was not arrogance at all. It was insecurity. That insecurity began to breed a form of paranoia." And he included Nixon as among the insecure.[clxv]

Illegal activities seemed to have begun in reaction to the release of the Pentagon Papers by Daniel Ellsberg, a full year before the Watergate break-in. Even though the revelations in these documents proved more damning of the Kennedy and Johnson administrations, the Nixon people determined that leaks of secrets like those of Ellsberg had to be stopped at all costs.

Nixon's Secretary of State Henry Kissinger was outraged by the publication of the Pentagon Papers and some historians feel that Kissinger's hatred of Ellsberg *sparked the whole thing*, meaning Watergate.[clxvi] Therefore, the president's men broke into Ellsberg's psychiatrist's office to seek embarrassing information about Ellsberg.

The Watergate break-in itself seemed a silly and misguided attempt to find information damaging to Democrats and possibly to find information the Democrats may have had that could prove damaging to the president. Once a crime has taken place, those involved must necessarily seek to prevent law enforcement and the public from finding out about it.

A cover-up of those crimes naturally ensued, and in this, Richard Nixon was directly complicit.

Again, from the Nixon memoir: "What really hurts in matters of this sort is not the fact that they occur, because overzealous people in campaigns do things that are wrong. What really hurts is if you try to cover it up."[clxvii]

But attempting to cover up he did. The reason we know this was because of the White House tapes, the existence of which became known during the Senate's Watergate hearings in 1973. On July 16, presidential aide Alexander Butterfield revealed the existence of the tapes to a stunned American public. It then appeared that the various allegations against the president could be confirmed by conversations on the tapes.

The taping system had been installed in the Nixon White House in February 1971. A similar system existed in the Johnson White House. John F. Kennedy recorded several conversations on tapes and Dictabelt recordings. There are various reasons why a president might want a taping system to exist. By having conversations recorded, the president has the ability to keep those he talks to honest, to have no question about what was said in a particular conversation. Politicians are known to make public statements at variance to what might have been said in private, and this would create an advantage for the president taping those private conversations. But they also preserve a record that would facilitate the writing of memoirs after the presidency, something that was clearly part of Nixon's motives. Whatever the case, the revelation of the existence of the taping system changed the entire Watergate matter.

During those Watergate hearings, bombshell revelations about the president's role in the cover-up had been made by former White House counsel John Dean. At first blush, Nixon felt the tapes could reveal Dean to be a liar. Dean testified about a meeting with the president on March 21, 1973 in which he described a *cancer on the presidency*, the cover-up that was being conducted by White House aides. The tapes would reveal that Nixon had told Dean they could raise the million dollars that Dean said might be necessary to keep the defendants quiet but "it would be wrong and it would not work."[clxviii]

Nixon wrote in his diary that payments were being made to the Watergate burglars and those who assisted them. Among the latter was E. Howard Hunt, a former CIA employee as well as a member of the White House staff. It was Nixon's hope that the money sent to them would lead them to plead guilty and avoid a trial. It was clear to him that the motive for these payments made the difference between what might be legal and what was clearly illegal. If the payments were made to "provide attorneys' fees and family support, then they were legal; if the purpose had been to buy silence from the defendants, that would be an obstruction of justice."[clxix] It became obvious to him that the payments would be a problem regardless of what the motive may have really been.

Theodore White, the historian made famous for the 'Making of the President' series that began with the 1960 campaign, wrote about how the tape contents reflected "the chaos inside the mind of Richard Nixon...they serpentine in and out of the President's conscience, his loyalty to his loyalists, his responsibilities, his vulnerability, their vulnerability, the principle of executive privilege, the political dimensions... The single thread that runs through them, if any thread can be found at all, is the thread of non-comprehension and his assumption of his own innocence. He had not, knew he had not, been guilty of ordering the Watergate break-in; his men had done that. But it was as if his chauffeur had been caught breaking a speed limit." White adds that instructions Nixon gave to Haldeman "to slow-up the FBI investigation...was of little moment as if he had tried to fix a police ticket for his chauffeur. And now it had all gotten out of hand; the details of what had happened led back to more details...and his mind apparently could not grasp what it all meant."

He goes on how to describe that as a lawyer, Nixon understood the principle that an official is guilty of a crime if he "should be able to recognize a crime but either fails to or refuses to bring it to court."[clxx]

On April 30, 1973, Nixon formally addressed the American people on the Watergate scandal. He announced that his two top aides, Robert Haldeman and John Ehrlichman, had resigned and that he had fired his counsel, John Dean. He later wrote in his memoir how, from that day forward, *the presidency lost all joy for me.* And he added that, had he been totally honest, he would have admitted that he had been a participant in an effort to cover up the crimes. He said in his speech that until the March 21 meeting with John Dean, he had no knowledge of the cover-up and repeated his assertion of personal innocence in the entire matter. He was hoping the public would continue to see that it was a matter typical in politics, as the polls showed. While he continued to talk about the important national matters that consumed him, that distracted him from concentrating on this as he should, he also wrote: "But these were still only excuses. They were not an accounting of my role. They were not explanations of how a President of the United States could so incompetently allow himself to get in such a situation. That was what people really wanted to know, and that was what my April 30 speech and all the other public statements I made about Watergate while I was president, failed to tell them."[clxxi]

The following month, on May 22, the White House issued a statement in an attempt to explain the myriad of stories that had come out during the Watergate investigation. Nixon admitted to wiretaps in 1969 designed to uncover the identities of those who were leaking national security secrets. He addressed the creation of the Plumbers, a cadre of operatives dispatched to plug those same leaks. These exposures were shocks to the American public, which made it harder to expect Nixon's protestations of innocence to resonate. He asserted that he had no intent or wish to impede the investigation in any way, and it was only in his own investigation that he learned about fundraising for the Watergate burglars. He had not authorized any offer of executive clemency for any of the defendants. Then, he writes in his memoir: "Thus, I set more traps that would be sprung by the tapes months later."[clxxii]

When the existence of the taping system was revealed on July 16, 1973, Nixon had several discussions about the tapes. He had actually told Haldeman two months earlier to destroy those tapes that didn't deal with national security events. Nonetheless, he found himself facing a decision about the future of the tapes. White House counsels Fred Buzhardt and Leonard Garment differed on the question. Buzhardt said they were Nixon's private property and should be destroyed. Garment, on the other hand, considered the tapes as evidence and, though he opposed releasing them, he felt strongly that they should not be destroyed.

After Chief of Staff Haldeman resigned, General Alexander Haig replaced him. Haig argued that destroying the tapes "would forever seal an impression of guilt in the public mind." Vice President Agnew felt they should be destroyed.

Even the First Lady Pat Nixon, hardly a first lady who was known by the public to express herself on any issues, had urged that her husband destroy the tapes.[clxxiii]

Nixon reflected that had he been a knowing Watergate conspirator, he would have recognized the problems the tapes would present and would have destroyed them. His reasoning for not doing so was based on many factors. "When I listened to them for the first time on June 4, 1973, I recognized that they were a mixed bag as far as I was concerned. There was politically embarrassing talk on them, and they contained many ambiguities, but I recognized that they indisputably disproved Dean's basic charge that I had conspired with him in an obstruction of justice over an eight-month period. I had not listened to the March 21 tape, but Haldeman had, and while I knew it would be difficult to explain in the critical and hostile atmosphere that now existed, he had told me that it could be explained, and I wanted to believe he was right."

He added, "If I had discussed illegal action, I would not have taped. If I had discussed illegal action and had taped, I would have destroyed the tapes once the investigation began."

On balance, he decided the tapes were his insurance policy against untrue charges that might be made against him, the "best insurance against the unforeseeable future, some protection in case people close to me would turn against me."[clxxiv]

He felt strongly that conversations inside the White House were protected by executive privilege, an undefined privilege at best and one that had not been tested in the courts. Candid conversations would never happen if those people involved felt their conversations might be later revealed. Just as conversations between a lawyer and a client are protected, private conversations with a president should be equally protected.

But he knew the desire from the Watergate Committee and most of his political adversaries would be for exposure of the tapes and that desire would be unrelenting. The effort he would mount to protect the tapes would consume the remainder of his presidency.

Because of the various members of the administration accused of being complicit in the lengthening Watergate investigation, Nixon reluctantly agreed to appoint a special prosecutor to oversee the investigation. To his chagrin, the special prosecutor sued for the release of tapes. He seemed to be facing challenges from all sides and desperately wanted to protect both the principle of executive privilege as well as the contents of the tapes.

And Watergate wasn't all he faced. Vice President Agnew had to resign in disgrace after being accused of taking bribes as Maryland's governor as well as vice president. Under the 25th amendment, for the first time, a vacancy in that office could be filled, which it was when Nixon selected Congressman Gerald Ford of Michigan for the post. By October 1973, the US Court of Appeals ruled against Nixon in a tapes case brought by the special prosecutor, Archibald Cox.

A compromise Nixon sought was, instead of releasing tapes, to have summaries of their contents released. Mississippi Democratic Senator John Stennis, a former judge, agreed with the president's request to review those summaries for accuracy. As Nixon feared, his opponents would have none of it. Among those who disagreed with the Stennis plan was special prosecutor Cox.

The controversy reached record levels on October 20 when Richard Nixon's patience ran out. He had Chief of Staff Haig tell Attorney General Elliot Richardson to fire Cox. Richardson refused and resigned from his office. His deputy, William Ruckelshaus, also refused the order and joined Richardson by resigning.

The third in command at the justice department, Solicitor General Robert Bork, fired Cox, and the administrative bloodletting that evening became known as the Saturday Night Massacre. Calls for Nixon's impeachment intensified.

The hunger for impeachment from many quarters was unprecedented in the United States. Organizations like the AFL-CIO, the ACLU, and consumer activists like Ralph Nader clamored for an end to the Nixon administration and the steady flow of information about crimes committed by its members. The House of Representatives judiciary committee would begin debating impeachment early in 1974. President Nixon faced all of this with the realization that the requests for more and more of the tapes would continue until all 5,000 hours were subpoenaed. He decided to draw the line by refusing to release more and continued to consider destroying those that had not been released. Among those that had been voluntarily released were conversations sought in a civil case brought by Ralph Nader. When it was learned that Nader's lawyer, William Dobrovir, had played the tapes at a Georgetown cocktail party, the outrage and anger felt by the president was impossible to measure. And among the multiple requests for more and more tapes from the special prosecutor and the House judiciary committee, many of those making the requests insisted that no further requests would be forthcoming, and Nixon dug in his heels.[clxxv]

By mid-April 1974, pollsters reported that a majority of the American public favored impeachment. White House lawyers sought an agreement with the president to compromise on the releasing of more tapes, but a decision was made to produce and make public transcripts of the tapes instead. With transcripts, sensitive material could legitimately be deleted but would embarrassing or illegal conversations be deleted as well? On April 29, Nixon addressed the public on TV to explain his decision to release transcripts only. He said, in part:

"I realize that these transcripts will provide grist for many sensational stories in the press. Parts will seem to be contradictory with one another and parts will be in conflict with some of the testimony given in the Senate Watergate Committee hearings.

I have been reluctant to release these tapes not just because they will embarrass me and those with whom I have talked – which they will – and not just because they will become the subject of speculation and even ridicule – which they will – and not just because certain parts of them will be seized upon by political and journalistic opponents – which they will.

I have been reluctant because, in these and all other conversations in this office, people have spoken their minds freely, never dreaming that specific sentences or even parts of sentences would be picked out as the subjects of national attention and controversy…

In giving you these records – blemishes and all – I am placing my trust in the basic fairness of the American people. I know in my own heart that through the long, painful, and difficult process revealed in these transcripts, I was trying in that period to discover what was right and to do what was right."[clxxvi]

The reaction throughout the country was not focused on the content revealed in the transcripts but more on the raw, bawdy language used by this most strait-laced of American leaders. No one imagined the number of spoken obscenities by the president that would be exposed in the transcripts, seemingly made more salacious by the phrase in many pages of the transcripts: *expletive deleted*. Support for him throughout the country peeled away even more. No shred of moral leadership remained.

On June 7, Nixon dictated diary entries that reviewed the series of missteps of which he had been guilty. He listed the hiring of Attorney General Richardson as his first mistake and then addressed "the bombshell of the tapes." After discussing it with Haig, Agnew had come to him, suggesting that he destroy the tapes. Nixon says, "Frankly, we thought about it. We should have done it."[clxxvii]

Leon Jaworski, appointed special prosecutor after the Cox firing, sued in federal court for the release of 64 new tapes. On May 20, the district court ruled in his favor and Nixon decided to petition the Supreme Court to hear his appeal of that decision. The drips and drabs of bad news that had come out from the tapes previously released would become a deluge if Jaworski was successful.

In June, President Nixon departed on a trip to the Middle East, to inject personal diplomacy into the never-ending effort to solve the Arab Israeli conflict. Many Americans saw his trip as a way to divert the country's attention from Watergate. He received a tumultuous reception in Egypt with more than a million people swarming the streets of Cairo to see him. He continued to be greeted by warm and friendly crowds in Saudi Arabia, Syria, Israel, and Jordan. These receptions were a stark contrast to the way he was being treated at home.

Shortly after returning home, Nixon left the country again, this time for another meeting with Russian leader Leonid Brezhnev in the Soviet Union, an event referred to as Summit III. During that trip, it also became known that he was fighting a dangerous ailment known as phlebitis, causing a painful swelling of his leg. It had been kept secret with Nixon fearing that he would be seen as *crippled mentally as well as physically*.[clxxviii]

By early July, Nixon was back in Washington and focused on the House judiciary committee's scheduled hearings on an impeachment resolution. His personal lobbying efforts changed no minds, and he became sure that the resolution would pass in the Democratic-controlled committee. Late one night during the last week of July, he wrote himself a note saying: "12:01 A.M. Lowest point in the presidency, and the Supreme Court still to come."[clxxix]

He didn't have long to wait. That same morning, July 24, the Supreme Court announced its unanimous decision in the case of *The United States v. Nixon*. His arguments for protecting executive privilege and his attempts to avoid releasing any more tapes had been rejected by the Court.

Within the tapes that would be released was a conversation Nixon had with Haldeman on June 23, 1972, in which they discussed using the CIA to get the FBI to limit its Watergate investigation for political reasons, not the national security reasons as Nixon had publicly stated.

This conversation would become known as the *smoking gun* and the end was near for the Nixon presidency.

Nixon's voice could be heard saying, "I don't give a shit what happens; I want you all to stonewall it, let them plead the Fifth Amendment, cover-up or anything else, if it'll save it, save the plan."[clxxx]

On July 27, the House judiciary committee voted 27-11 to impeach President Nixon for obstruction of justice. Two more articles were to be similarly passed. It was the first time a Congressional body had voted for an impeachment of a president since the presidency of Andrew Johnson, more than a hundred years before.

When the June 23rd tape was released, whatever support the president thought he could count on went away. He reached a decision to resign and became convinced it was the right decision after a final meeting with Republican Congressional leaders.

House Republican leader John Rhodes, Senate Republican leader Hugh Scott, and the 1964 GOP standard-bearer and Republican patriarch in the Senate, Barry Goldwater, met with President Nixon at the White House and told him that he would not survive an impeachment vote in either house of Congress.

On August 8, Nixon addressed the nation from the Oval Office and announced he would resign effective noon the following day. Vice President Gerald Ford would be sworn in at that time.

The largest scandal in American history was rapidly coming to its end. In all, 41 government officials were indicted and convicted of crimes relating to Watergate. Those high administration officials who served time in prison for their crimes included former Chief of Staff H.R. Haldeman, former Domestic Affairs Advisor John Erlichman, former White House Legal Counselor John Dean, former Attorney General John Mitchell, and former Special Counsel to the President Charles Colson. Former White House staff members directly involved in the break-in at the Democratic National Committee, E. Howard Hunt and G. Gordon Liddy, were also jailed.

Since his resignation from the presidency was likely the worst thing Richard Nixon could have imagined, would it have happened if he had destroyed the tapes before they became public knowledge? The public outrage after their existence was made public would have been intense but could it have been worse than the revelations of what was on the tapes?

Had they been destroyed before the public knew about them, the outrage surely would have been less. Many people would have felt strongly that getting rid of the tapes was an obstruction of justice, but would the result have been worse for Nixon than it was? It would have been far easier for his supporters to fight for Nixon if the contents and language in the tapes had never been revealed.

A little more than two and a half years after the resignation, Richard Nixon participated in a series of interviews with British television personality David Frost. Frost posed the question to the former president; why didn't he burn the tapes?

Nixon discussed his recollection that he had asked Haldeman to destroy those tapes that didn't have historical value, particularly in the area of national security and foreign affairs. When he learned how the taping system worked, by automatically turning on when activated by voices, he had wanted to change that so the system would only operate by being consciously turned on or off. He repeated his assertion, after the John Dean testimony before the Watergate Committee, that the tapes contradicted Dean. He stated, "I didn't feel there was a reason to destroy them."

Before their existence became public, he didn't feel they would come out, but if they did, their contents wouldn't have hurt him. But, as the conversation went on, he concluded that burning the tapes might have meant avoiding the resignation. Had he thought anything they revealed would be criminal, "I sure as the dickens would have destroyed them."

Bob Woodward and Carl Bernstein were the two *Washington Post* reporters who unraveled the entire Watergate scandal. After Nixon's resignation, they wrote a book about his last days in the White House called *The Final Days*. They interviewed former White House counsel Leonard Garment, who had advised Nixon not to destroy the tapes. Garment told them why Nixon decided not to burn the tapes, in effect, "that Nixon wanted the world to see the ugliness of his mind"…that "Nixon wanted the world to see him go to the bathroom." Fawn Brodie adds that while Nixon "promised to bring us 'truth in government'…By not destroying the tapes he had brought us the worst of the truth about himself. The tapes meant his political destruction, the ruin of his reputation, the annihilation of the fantasy image of the good, decent, law-abiding president."[clxxxi]

One of the Nixon White House aides who continued to work with him in his post-presidency was Diane Sawyer. After that experience, she went to work for CBS and became a successful and famous newswoman. In 1982, she conducted an interview with the former president and surprised him with her probing questions about Watergate.

She asked him point blank why he didn't burn the tapes. The response was, "I've covered that also, of course, in my – memoirs, and I must say that if – I must get – I must get – oh, a half a dozen letters a week even now. 'Why didn't you burn those tapes?' And the answer is, of course, I should. It should have been done. But the main part is, they should never have been started."[clxxxii]

Also in 1982, Nixon gave an interview with the magazine *Family Weekly*. He acknowledged that he should have burned the tapes and thought he was very naïve not to have destroyed them. But he added, "The tapes were put in there for the purpose of being available to the Presidential Library for historical reasons." As if to justify them, he went on to recount how Eisenhower, Kennedy, and Johnson all had their own taping systems in the White House. Then Nixon laughed and, "as if suddenly struck by the absurdity of his rationale. 'But I suppose that's the last taping there will be'."[clxxxiii]

Resignation or impeachment were the worst possible results for Richard Nixon. It is impossible to know if either of them would have happened if the contents of the tapes had never become public. Burning them would have led to a charge of obstruction of justice but it can't be assumed that the charge would have led to impeachment.

In the years that followed, the public has become increasingly familiar with the language used by Nixon in the privacy of the office. The tapes revealed language that was not only profane but showed him to be bigoted, paranoid, racist, and antisemitic. Had he known what the tapes would have meant to his legacy, he would have surely destroyed them. The decision not to do so was certainly, from Richard Nixon's standpoint, a bad one.

George H. W. Bush – Courtesy of the George H.W. Bush Presidential Library and Museum

George H.W. Bush – Read My Lips

George Herbert Walker Bush, America's 41st president, was about as well prepared to be president as anyone ever had been. His resume compared to only a few others in American history.

John Quincy Adams, America's sixth president, traveled with his father, who would become America's second president, to foreign diplomatic posts as a youth during an era when the vast majority of his fellow citizens never left the country's shores. He would first be elected to the Massachusetts State Senate at age 34, and a year later, was elected to the United States Senate. Prior to elective office, he served as minister to the Netherlands and then to Prussia. After the U.S. Senate, he would become minister to Russia and then the United Kingdom. Adams served as secretary of state for eight consecutive years under President James Monroe and is considered one of the most accomplished secretaries of state of all time. Secretary of state was then considered the steppingstone to the presidency, which was where he ended up.

James Buchanan, the nation's 15th president, was elected to the Pennsylvania House of Representatives at age 23 and followed up by being elected to the U.S. House of Representatives. After 10 years in Congress, he became the minister to Russia during the presidency of Andrew Jackson. Returning home, he was elected to the U.S. Senate. After 10 years in the Senate, he was appointed secretary of state by President James Polk, followed by an appointment to be minister to the United Kingdom by President Franklin Pierce. His election to be president was only eight months after returning from England.

Herbert Hoover became America's 31st president after serving in a number of high-profile posts and earning himself an international reputation. Before the United States entered World War I, he served as chairman of the Commission for Relief in Belgium. The war had brought about a food crisis in Belgium, and he helped feed millions of starving war victims. After America's entry into the war, he was appointed by President Woodrow Wilson to be the director of the United States Food Administration, to help ensure America's food needs during the conflict. After the war, he continued to direct the efforts to feed starving Europeans. Just as he had been successful in his private life prior to public service, he showed himself skilled in these posts as well. He was appointed the country's third secretary of Commerce by President Warren Harding and served throughout the Harding and Calvin Coolidge administrations until deciding to seek the presidency himself in 1928.

George Bush's resume would compare to that of Adams, Buchanan, and Hoover. Born into a wealthy family in Connecticut with a political pedigree, his father would be a U.S. senator. Bush would distinguish himself in World War II then move to Texas to make his own way in the oil business. He was elected to the U.S. House of Representatives at age 42 and served there for four years before being appointed U.S. Ambassador to the United Nations by President Richard Nixon. He served there for two years until President Nixon asked him to take over the reins as chair of the Republican National Committee. He served there throughout the Watergate scandal, managing to keep his own reputation intact. When Nixon resigned and Gerald Ford became president, Bush was asked to become the country's 2nd chief of the U.S. Liaison Office to the People's Republic of China. U.S.-China diplomatic relations had only recently been re-established, and his role was, in effect, the ambassador. After serving barely more than a year in China, President Ford asked him to take over as director of the Central Intelligence Agency.

After a year at the CIA, Bush decided to seek the presidency himself and was defeated for the nomination by the former California Governor Ronald Reagan. Reagan chose Bush to be his vice-presidential running mate, and they were elected in 1980. Bush served as vice president for the full two terms of the Reagan presidency then successfully sought the presidency in 1988.

These four men in American history had backgrounds and credentials that are hard to match in the ranks of other American presidents. And they all have one thing in common.

Each was a one-term president.

To err is human and it was the errors of these four men that resulted in them being denied a second term in the White House. John Quincy Adams had been part of what became known as the *corrupt bargain*. It was a deal he made with the Speaker of the House Henry Clay, one of his opponents in the presidential race of 1824. Clay threw his support to Adams in return for an appointment as secretary of state. That deal tarnished the Adams presidency and fueled the efforts of Andrew Jackson to take the presidency four years later.

James Buchanan faced the divisive era leading up to the Civil War. His inability to manage the conflict in a manner that might avoid war led to his demise. This most competent of public servants will forever be linked to a presidency marked by its incompetency. He made no effort to keep the southern states from seceding and turned the presidency over to Abraham Lincoln, perhaps America's greatest president.

Herbert Hoover was president during the greatest economic crisis the country had ever experienced. He had been president less than eight months when the stock market crashed and the American economy, even the worldwide economy, spiraled down into the Great Depression. Hoover was philosophically opposed to an activist federal government and shied away from taking steps that might have relieved the crisis. In the eyes of most Americans, he fiddled while Rome burned and did little to ease the pain the country was experiencing. The woes of the nation increased while the American people saw little effort by their president to do anything about it. His inactivity led to the landslide election of his activist Democratic opponent, Franklin D. Roosevelt.

Of these four men, Bush was the only one who was vice president. And a vice president hadn't been elected to the presidency since Martin Van Buren in 1836. As the office of secretary of state seemed to be a steppingstone to the White House, at least in the country's 1st century, the vice presidency clearly was not.

The bad decision that led to George Bush's one-term presidency concerned taxes. There were a number of issues facing him as he sought the presidency. As Ronald Reagan's vice president, he needed Reagan supporters to see him as a worthy successor. Reagan had faced a scandal involving arms for hostages, known as Iran-Contra, and Bush was very much politically affected by the controversy. He seemed to know more than he admitted but since he had never been viewed as a decision-maker in the matter, the issue didn't seem to affect his fortunes much.

What seemed to affect him more was his patrician image as compared to the former actor Ronald Reagan; the public was familiar with his scenes from Westerns and his manly clearing of brush on his ranch. The issue came to a head on October 19, 1987, when it was clear that Vice President Bush would be seeking the presidency. *Newsweek* magazine published its cover story with the title, *George Bush: Fighting the Wimp Factor.*

While most people felt the title to be unfair and a smear, there is no question it had an impact. It was revealed in later years that the reporter writing the story, Margaret Garrard Warner, objected to the title, and *Newsweek's* editor, Evan Thomas, expressed regret for it.

It is easy to imagine how certain postures and public positions might be taken to make him appear more manly than he was considered to be by the press, if not by the public. Perception in politics is far more important than reality and George Bush must have bristled at this portrayal of him as a wimp. This was the man who had become a combat pilot at age 18 and flew 58 missions. He had won the Distinguished Flying Cross. He had served as America's chief spy when he headed the CIA. How could he possibly be seen as a wimp? Yet the press kept printing a "spate of jokes, cartoons, and anecdotes" that seemed to reveal the "candidate's wimpiness." Before he chose a running mate in 1988, there were rumors that he would choose United Nations Ambassador Jeane Kirkpatrick, an anti-Communist hard-liner, to lend *some machismo* to the ticket.[clxxxiv]

All of these factors seemed to contribute to a requirement that he needed to be tough. Making a definitive statement that he would stand by the American people in the face of all his political advisors to prevent any tax increase would be one way. The most public expression of this posture would be made in a way that evoked Clint Eastwood's tough guy Dirty Harry from several movies. Facing a bad guy reaching for a gun, Harry the cop aimed his own gun and spat out, "Go ahead…Make my day."

When Reagan, who loved making movie references, was facing off with Democrats over taxes and was threatening a veto, he used the exact Dirty Harry quote.[clxxxv]

When Reagan ran for president, his tough-guy stance was enhanced by his vehemence about the Soviet Union. Referring to it as the *Evil Empire* scared a lot of people at the time, worried that his saber-rattling could have dire consequences.

But, by the time George Bush sought the presidency, relations with the Soviet Union had cooled precipitously, mainly because of the summit meetings

Reagan held with the new Soviet leader, Mikhail Gorbachev. It wasn't the time for tough talking about the Soviets.

Anti-tax sentiment was also central to the philosophy of many in the Republican Party. Pandering to that wing would always be a temptation, but as America faced economic reality in late 1988, the deficit had become a major issue. Most pundits would describe the Democratic Party as the big-spending, tax-increasing party.

The Republicans used that label and worked hard to oppose government spending and tax increases. Yet Reagan had raised taxes in 1982, seriously disappointing his most strident adherents.

Despite that and the scandal that swirled around him, Ronald Reagan was quite popular when he ended his second term. Polls showed him at a 68% approval ranking nationally with a 90% approval among Republicans. It was a great environment for his vice president to seek the presidency.[clxxxvi]

George Bush, by all accounts, was a man who believed in public service and was known by intimates to look at every issue with an eye toward what was best for America. He entered the presidency much more engaged in issue details than his predecessor and continued to be serious about doing the right thing.

He was raised to take public service seriously and demonstrated it throughout his life. In later years, he was quoted as saying, "public servants have an obligation to try to leave the earth better than we found it."[clxxxvii]

Yet, at a critical juncture in his political life, he announced a decision that not only seemed to be pandering to part of his base that would seriously affect not only his presidency but his legacy as well. It would handcuff him as president and provide fodder to his political enemies.

So, the questions are: why did he make such a decision, what was its impact, and was it a bad decision?

When he announced his candidacy for president on October 13, 1987, he said, "I am not going to raise your taxes – period," which seemed to be a reaction to a Reagan tax hike in 1982 and his increases in social security deductions.[clxxxviii] It was a way of separating himself from Reagan while doing something that would appeal to the Reagan die-hards, of which there were many. As the campaign rolled on, Bush told others that he saw himself as a blank slate as he approached the Republican National Convention, and it would be a time for his *declaration of being*, yet he didn't state a different approach on the tax issue; he raised the ante.[clxxxix]

During the campaign, Bush was told by his economic advisors that "higher taxes might be necessary to reduce the federal deficit." When asked about this, Bush told reporters, "I just simply said I was not going to propose a tax increase."[cxc] What made this more difficult was a law then in effect that required deficit reduction, the Gramm-Rudman-Hollings Act, and Reagan policies had expanded the deficit substantially. Reagan's economic policies, known as *supply-side*, proposed lower taxes with a huge increase in defense spending and the budget was more unbalanced than ever before. "Obligations stood at nearly $2.7 trillion…serving the debt came to $200 billion annually." [cxci] The $2.7 trillion debt had been $1 trillion when Reagan took office. If taxes weren't to be raised at all, the only way to reduce the deficit would be by cutting entitlements.

Underscoring the importance of deficit reduction is a quote from the former head of the Congressional Budget Office, Alice Rivlin: "The budget deficit has become a defense issue, a foreign policy issue, a health-care issue, an education issue. Getting the budget deficit behind us has become a test of our ability to govern."[cxcii]

An important Bush aide was Dick Darman, who came to him as the deputy of James Baker, who had been Reagan's chief of staff and then secretary of the Treasury. Darman expressed grave concerns about the no-tax stance, arguing that Bush would be locking himself into a box. But Bush insisted on his position and wanted it strongly articulated at the convention.

In his speech, he said, "The Congress will push me to raise taxes, and I'll say no. And they'll push, and I'll say no. And they'll push again, and I'll say to them, read my lips: no new taxes."[cxciii]

That was about as firm as he could be. Polls after the convention showed him either tied or ahead of Democratic candidate Michael Dukakis.

Bush won the election but even before his inauguration, advisors started bringing up the need for new taxes. Incoming Treasury Secretary Nick Brady and pollster Robert Teeter, at a meeting in the vice president's residence, "seemed to be leaning toward accepting the need for new taxes." But Bush held firm.[cxciv]

In a *Time* magazine article written just after the inauguration, the famous quote was described as "a politically expedient stance that helped him win election and now threatens his ability to govern successfully." A senior administration official was quoted as saying, "Backing off that promise could destroy his presidency. But we'll probably have to do just that. How we do it without making the President out to be a liar or an incompetent weakling is going to take all of George Bush's skills. The shiftiness required to get out of that box is going to make everything he's done to get here seem like child's play."[cxcv]

During the first year of Bush's presidency, agreement was reached on a budget for fiscal year 1990 with no new taxes. But Dick Darman, the new director of the Office of Management and the Budget, feared that new taxes would be necessary in fiscal year 1991. The bipartisanship that Bush needed to pass the FY1990 budget would be more difficult if taxes were truly needed in addition to more severe cuts in entitlements. And those would have to be considered in an election year.

Darman knew what he was talking about. Before Bush had completed two full years in office, he signed off on a compromise with Congressional Democrats that included raising taxes. The deficit, it was feared, would likely bring on a recession, and facing tax increases might be less damaging than facing the electorate during a recession.[cxcvi]

While Bush was wrestling with an international issue after Iraq's Saddam Hussein invaded Kuwait, he was also negotiating with a bi-partisan group of Congressional leaders to come up with a budget that would reduce the deficit. The nation was facing a potential deficit of $300 billion for the fiscal year, which Bush described as *the cancer* of deficits. But Republicans who felt he was reneging on his no-tax pledge deserted him and his budget failed in the House.

William F. Buckley editorialized in the *National Review*: "Ronald Reagan was often denounced for being divisive, but it was precisely because he was divisive that the American people saw that, in the contest between Us and Them, The Gipper was one of Us. In the last six months, the signal President Bush has sent is that he is a *Them*."[cxcvii]

After several more days of negotiating, the Omnibus Budget Reconciliation Act of 1990 was passed, which included an income tax increase. Only one-quarter of the Republicans in both houses of Congress backed the president.[cxcviii] Bush had created his own Achilles heel as he looked

139

toward a re-election campaign in 1992. But first, as it turned out, he would have to fight for the nomination.

Former Reagan communications director, who had established a successful television career and gained a reputation as a died-in-the-wool conservative, was Patrick Buchanan. Buchanan entered the New Hampshire primary against Bush. Central to the Buchanan campaign was the fact that Bush had gone back on his no tax pledge. His brochures read, "We will keep the promises George Bush broke." Bush and much of the American political establishment were shocked when Buchanan garnered over 37% of the vote in the first-in-the-nation New Hampshire primary, trailing Bush by only 16%.

For an incumbent president, this was a poor showing and fueled the independent candidacy in the fall of millionaire businessman Ross Perot. The Democratic nominee would be Arkansas Governor Bill Clinton, whose campaign would include a devastating ad mocking the Bush pledge.

At the Democratic Convention, Clinton included the following in his speech: "Four years ago, he promised 15 million new jobs by this time, and he's over 14 million short... The incumbent President says unemployment always goes up a little before recovery begins, but unemployment only has to go up one more person before a real recovery can begin. And Mr. President, you are that man."[cxcix]

Bush, on the other hand, when he addressed the Republican Convention acknowledged that he had made a mistake "in signing the deficit-reduction bill with its gas-tax hike and that, if re-elected, he'd cut taxes again." Pivoting to a more personal attack on the Democratic nominee who had famously avoided going to the Vietnam War, he contrasted his World War II experience with Clinton's opposition to the war by declaring, "While I bit the bullet, he bit his nails."[cc]

In that speech, Bush accused Clinton of raising taxes 128 times as governor of Arkansas and *enjoying it every time*. Major American newspapers described the charge as misleading; it included fees on beauty pageants, court costs for convicted criminals, and a requirement that used-car dealers post a $25,000 bond. Even conservative columnist George Will wrote that, "by the President's criteria, 'Bush has raised taxes more often in four years than Clinton has in ten'."[cci]

On election day, Perot was able to win almost 19% of the vote, preventing any of the candidates from winning a popular vote majority. In fact, the only state to give a majority of its popular votes to any candidate was Clinton's Arkansas. Clinton won an electoral vote majority but only 43% of the popular vote. One can only speculate on the impact that the Bush pledge had on the election outcome.

When George Bush died in 2018, an NPR commentary about his life said the following about his "Read my lips" quote. Under the heading "It helped…then probably hurt" was the following:

'Read my lips' succeeded, probably beyond their fondest dreams. Polls showed that after the convention, Bush had a lead over Democrat Michael Dukakis. But if it improved Bush's chances of being elected that year, it may also have ruined his chances of being re-elected in 1992.

That was because less than two years after making the no-tax pledge, Bush found himself in circumstances in which he no longer felt he could keep it. Locked in budget negotiations with the majority Democrats in the House and Senate, Bush felt he had to allow higher rates on some existing taxes or the Gramm-Rudman deficit-reduction bill would shut down important services of the government.

So he signed off on a compromise involving revenues as well as spending restraints. Democrats exulted at having forced him to renege. Conservatives seethed. A young Newt Gingrich, elevated to the No. 2 spot in the House Republican leadership the previous year, made no secret of his displeasure. He insisted any option was preferable to any new revenue.

That position helped inspire a major Republican challenger to Bush's renomination in 1992. He was Patrick Buchanan, a former communications director for Reagan and a familiar commentator on TV. He announced his campaign for president in December 1991, saying he was running "because, we Republicans, can no longer say it is all the liberals' fault. It was not some liberal Democrat who said, 'Read my lips: no new taxes', then broke his word to cut a seedy backroom budget deal with the big spenders on Capitol Hill."[ccii]

On the 35th anniversary of the statement by President Nixon saying, "I am not a crook," *Time* Magazine printed a list of the *Top 10 Unfortunate Political One-Liners*,[cciii] of which the Nixon comment was number one. Second place went to Bill Clinton's "I did not have sexual relations with that woman" with "Read my lips: no new taxes" coming in third.

Thirty years after "Read my lips," *Time* magazine would characterize Bush's pledge. The "quote helped Bush defeat Michael Dukakis, became a cornerstone of his Saturday Night Live persona (embodied by Dana Carvey), and also caught him in a political snare. At a time of major budget deficits and spending needs, Bush was – as many had predicted – unable to get by with cuts alone. Before his first year in office was complete, he signed into law a 'stealth budget' that, while leaving the income tax alone, raised various fees and levies. In 1990, David Letterman was joking that Bush's catchphrase should be updated to 'Read my lips: I was lying'; sure enough, it was clear that the original promise had to go... But, though the promise itself proved impossible to keep, George H.W. Bush's words themselves have had a longevity far beyond their time."[cciv]

President Bill Clinton and Vice President Al Gore, Jr. – Courtesy National Archives and Record Administration

Al Gore – Keep Away

Al Gore had been vice president for the two terms of the Bill Clinton presidency when he was nominated by the Democratic Party to run for president in 2000.

He lost one of the closest elections in history to Texas Governor George W. Bush. While winning the popular vote by half a million votes, he lost the Electoral College by only five votes, 271 to 266. Since the smallest state has three electoral votes, winning any state in the country that he lost would have changed the results for Gore and the country.

Conventional thinking says that Gore should have been elected. The state of the economy is almost always the predominant issue in presidential elections. As Bill Clinton described the economic environment in 2000; there was a budget surplus of $200 billion, a 10-year projected surplus of over $400 trillion, and the economy had produced 22 million jobs during the life of the Clinton administration.

The budget had been balanced, and the economy was in great shape.[ccv] And, Bill Clinton was enormously popular, with some pollsters reporting that his job approval ratings were over 70% with others rating his popularity in the low 60s.

But there was another issue lurking behind the scenes of American politics as it turned its attention toward the presidential election. In December 1998, Bill Clinton became only the second president in American history to be impeached by the House of Representatives.

He was charged with lying about an affair he had with White House intern Monica Lewinsky. The impeachment process itself was viewed by the American public as partisan and the matter hardly dented his popularity. He was acquitted by the Senate in 1999 and remained popular with the electorate.

When asked by reporters if Al Gore was being tarnished by the scandal, Clinton responded that he saw no evidence of that, that the public wasn't holding Gore responsible for mistakes that he, Clinton, had made.

He added that he "knew three things about Al Gore: he had had a more positive impact on our country as vice president than any of his predecessors; he had the right positions on the issues and would keep the prosperity going; and he understood the future, both its possibilities and its dangers. I believed if all the voters understood that, Al would win."[ccvi]

Vice President Albert Gore, Jr. was personally offended by President Bill Clinton's behavior that led to the Lewinski scandal. Despite the fact that Clinton was enormously popular, Gore decided to avoid appearing with Clinton and basically stayed away from him during the campaign. Given the closeness of the election result, this decision can be credited with causing Gore's loss.

Terry McAuliffe, a close friend of Clinton who would later become chair of the Democratic National Committee and then governor of Virginia, described how the centerpiece of the Gore campaign should have been the peace and prosperity of the eight years of the Clinton presidency, of which Gore was a major part. Instead, because of the Monica Lewinsky scandal, Gore inexplicably separated himself from Clinton and kept him at arm's length through the campaign.

"Not using Clinton also created a negative image for the Gore campaign. The decision raised questions about why he was being held at arm's length, which opened the door for Bush to run as a so-called compassionate conservative who would restore dignity and honor to the White House." He goes on to describe how easy it was to assume that Bill Clinton's campaigning could have meant "7,211 more votes in New Hampshire or 537 more votes in Florida," either of which would have won the election for Gore. Easier yet is to assume that Clinton's campaigning could have made a difference in Clinton's home state of Arkansas, which Bush won and also could have made the difference.

The Democratic base needed to be fired up, but Gore's people seemed to concentrate instead on swing voters; Gore needed to do a better job of *firing up his base*. Bill Clinton could have done that for the Democrats.[ccvii]

Albert Gore, Jr. was a very different person than Bill Clinton. While Clinton had been born into a hard scrabble life in Arkansas to a widowed mother, who would remarry shortly before Clinton turned four, he was not a child of privilege in any manner. Gore, on the other hand, would be born into a famous Tennessee family.

His mother Pauline had been one of the first women to graduate from Vanderbilt University Law School, and his father Albert Gore, Sr., was a member of Congress, elected to the House of Representatives before Al Jr. was born and would be elected to the U.S. Senate when Al Jr. was five years old.

Much of Al Gore Jr's life would be spent living in the Fairfax Hotel in Washington, DC's embassy row. The Gores would be seen, especially by the Clintons, as Washington insiders. A governor of Arkansas would hardly be described that way.

Al Gore was, in the words of Creedence Clearwater Revival, a "Fortunate Son." Bill Clinton, on the other hand, would identify with the lyrics saying, "I ain't no senator's son."

Where Bill Clinton was a natural politician, gifted with the ability to make people he was talking with feel as if they were the only people in the room, Al Gore was quieter, more cerebral, more interested in issues than the backslapping of politics. This is not to suggest Clinton wasn't smart; he had been a Rhode Scholar.

Gore's intelligence showed through more by his deliberate nature in conversation, a scholarly demeanor. But he also described himself as "one of the most introverted people in public life."[ccviii]

No one would describe Bill Clinton as introverted. Where Clinton was nicknamed *Slick Willie*, Gore was referred to as *Dudley Do-Right*.[ccix]

In 2009, *Politico* published an article with an interesting description of these two men:

"They were, and are, deeply different personalities. With his once-in-a-generation political skills and effortless gift of gab, Clinton never quite got Gore's brainy awkwardness and seeming inability to totally master the basic stagecraft of running for office. For his part, Gore, by numerous accounts, was horrified by Clinton's lack of discipline, an irritation that grew to near-revulsion when the details of his affair with Lewinsky finally became public.

There is also the clash of southern archetypes in the Clinton-Gore saga – a clash that has often echoed in the lives of both men. Clinton, for all his tours through Oxford, New Haven, and ultimately Washington, is at his heart a lower-middle class kid from Hot Springs, Ark. He saw Gore, the son of Tennessee who actually grew up in Washington as the son of a senator, as a quintessential elitist. As Clinton once said of another stiff Southern politician who has stayed too long in the North: 'He'd ask for Chablis at a fish fry."[ccx]

Both men were born in 1948 and when they joined together as a team in 1992, the Democratic ticket for president and vice president, a natural friendship seemed to develop as well as a solid political partnership. As they campaigned together with their wives, Hillary Clinton and Tipper Gore, the friendship deepened. At one point, Tipper described Hillary as her "long-lost sister."

By all accounts, Clinton brought Gore into the operations of his administration to a greater extent than most, if not all, presidents in American history. It was a true partnership. But the partnership included Hillary as well, often the recipient of responsibilities that had never been given a first lady and might otherwise have been given to Gore.

The first public evidence of the substantive role that would be assumed by the new first lady was when she was assigned to be head of the healthcare task force. It wouldn't take long before the White House staff came to understand that major decisions required sign-off by the president, vice president, and first lady.[ccxi]

A close Clinton friend and advisor was quoted as saying, "Al Gore hasn't yet realized there is going to be a co-presidency but he's not going to be part of the co," and that Gore "would have to adjust to a smaller role."

It might be natural for a vice president, especially a young VP like Gore, to see himself as the president's successor. But it soon became clear that many Clinton intimates saw Hillary in that role.[ccxii]

Yet, Al Gore cemented a close relationship with Clinton; both of them cared deeply about issues and would lunch weekly to discuss the intricacies of those matters facing the administration.

One author characterized the relationship by writing that "Bill's panoramic but haphazard intelligence often benefited from Gore's more rigorous and linear thinking."[ccxiii]

Six years into the presidency, 1998, represented a volcanic shift in the three relationships. Early that year the Lewinsky affair was revealed. Bill Clinton, in an effort to protect his presidency and his marriage as well as to avoid public embarrassment, lied about the affair. His lies under oath in a deposition would lead to his impeachment but he also lied to his wife and his vice president, among others.

Most Americans seemed to understand why a man would lie about an illicit sexual affair, especially one outside of the marriage, and Bill Clinton remained extremely popular. But that was not the way Hillary Clinton and Al Gore reacted.

When New York Senator Daniel Patrick Moynihan announced in November that he would not be running for re-election in 2000, Hillary decided to make the race. As Al Gore began planning for a presidential run of his own, Hillary had a new set of priorities, and Bill was a lame-duck president facing scandal and impeachment.

Bill Clinton's priorities would be first to survive impeachment but then to support his wife in her bid to be a United States senator. Helping his vice president succeed him would be next in line. During 1999, Clinton's priorities became clear. Bill and Hillary appeared together at 20 White House-oriented public events while Al Gore was included in one, an event that also featured Tipper and both Clintons.

From campaign polling, Gore could see, however, that the country had grown weary of the Clinton scandal as well as the drumbeat of allegations brought against them by a collection of right-wing organizations. He could also note that his own popularity had fallen during the year of the Lewinsky scandal.

When he announced his candidacy on June 16, 1999, the Clintons were out of the country. Gore referred to Clinton only twice.

That evening in a television interview, he was asked about the Lewinsky affair. "I thought it was awful. I thought it was inexcusable. But I made a commitment to serve this country as vice president…as a father," he thought, Clinton's behavior "was terribly wrong, obviously…it is our own lives we must master if we are to have the moral authority to guide our children."

Bill Clinton was not happy about what he heard in the interview but didn't share his feelings with Gore, instead praised him in a phone call. Similarly, Gore expressed outrage at Clinton's behavior in private, but not to the president directly.[ccxiv]

There was a natural competition between Hillary Clinton and Al Gore, not just the time spent in White House events or space on the White House website, but in the area of fundraising as well. Gore would have liked Hillary campaigning for him, which wasn't happening, but had real concerns about the number of fundraisers and donors who had gravitated to her and not to him.

Bill Clinton did headline two fundraisers for Gore in the fall of 1999. As the election year arrived, observers noted that Bill was appearing at Hillary's fundraisers as well but not doing other public events for either candidate.

What was becoming clear to Clinton staffers was that the president wanted to be the centerpiece of attention in a Gore campaign and considered Gore ungrateful when he understood that was not to be. He bristled at the thought that he could be politically radioactive. If it hadn't been for him, neither Hillary nor Al would be embarking on the efforts currently underway.

Journalist Sally Bedell Smith wrote, *"For all his praise of Al Gore in scores of speeches, Bill's behavior throughout 2000 – making passive-aggressive remarks, belittling Gore in private, grabbing the spotlight with his own political star turns, and continuing to argue his innocence in various scandals – betrayed ambivalence about a Gore victory, at least one earned on the vice president's own terms."*[ccxv]

Tensions increased between the Gore and Clinton camps as Gore moved to separate himself from the president. He was focused on those parts of the electorate put off by the Clinton scandal and personally abhorred the president's immorality. During the campaign, the weekly lunches stopped. "In the absence of personal contact their misunderstandings multiplied, and they became, if not estranged from each other, at least disaffected."[ccxvi]

Al Gore's efforts to separate himself were often made difficult in ways he couldn't prevent. When he would be nominated at the Democratic National Convention, there was no way to keep the president away. But not only did Bill Clinton address the convention, Hillary did as well. Worse yet, a few days before the convention, Bill publicly spoke in a church, talking about himself as a sinner.

He said that he had publicly apologized for his mistakes, had nothing left to hide, and was well into "the second year of a process of trying to totally rebuild my life."[ccxvii] In Clinton's memoir, he described the speech as a welcome and non-political event, seemingly oblivious to its political impact.[ccxviii] Al Gore didn't need this loud confessional at that particular moment.

As Gore faced off against George W. Bush, he was constantly reminded how difficult it was to separate himself, as Bush consistently referred to the Clinton-Gore administration, implicitly linking *him to the president's scandals*. Bill Clinton's well-known conduct was, in the words of a Gore consultant, "the elephant in the living room."[ccxix]

This comment infuriated many Clinton advisors, according to *The Washington Post*. One snarky response was, "I don't think the fact that they lost four out of four debates had anything to do with Bill Clinton." Although there were periodic reports of their tension during the campaign, a Democrat close to both men said, "It was far worse than anyone knew."[ccxx]

The president, however, wanted to be involved in the Gore campaign and communicated regularly with campaign officials to make sure his interest was known. He asked the campaign if he could hit the road for Gore over the last few weeks and was told no.[ccxxi] But while he was expressing frustration about being shut out, he would make unhelpful comments about Gore. He would voice criticisms that had a real impact on Gore's unfavorable ratings. This behavior didn't ease the tensions, especially when polls showed Gore's *honesty and forthrightness* lagged far behind those of Bush. To make matters worse, consumer advocate Ralph Nader had entered the race as an independent, generating fears that most of his votes would come from Gore and not Bush.[ccxxii]

The victory of George W. Bush in the 2000 election is a complicated story in and of itself. There were inconsistent predictions, or calls, of the television networks on election night. The Florida election result, first called for Gore, then switched away from him, became a national drama that stretched out for weeks. Confusing ballots, long recounts, and then a case to stop the recount that went before the Supreme Court. The Court decided to stop the recount in a manner that gave the Florida election to Bush, pushing him over the top by the slimmest of margins.

As it turned out, the fears about Nader's impact were warranted. Gore lost New Hampshire by 7,000 votes while Nader garnered over 22,000. The Florida recount was stopped when the margin was only 537 votes for Bush. Nader had won over 97,000 votes.

Sally Bedell Smith wrote about the Clinton White House years in which she described the election this way: "Even though he had received far more votes and a higher percentage than Bill Clinton had in his two presidential races, Gore found himself battling accusations from the Clinton camp that if the president had been unleashed on the campaign trail he would have energized the Democratic base and enabled Gore to win." She goes on to quote a Gore consultant who insisted that Clinton wasn't the only reason they lost, but there was no question they would have won had it not been for the Lewinsky scandal.[ccxxiii]

Clinton and Gore remained angry with each other, finally confronting the matter in an Oval Office meeting on December 21. It was not pleasant, with Gore blaming the scandals while Clinton rebuked him for failing to rely on their successful administration.[ccxxiv] *The Washington Post* described the meeting: "…people close to both have described its tone in similar language. *Tense* was the description of one adviser to Clinton, while a Gore aide called it *cathartic*. One Democrat who has worked closely with both men called the session *very, very blunt*."[ccxxv]

Author Taylor Branch, a close Clinton friend, interviewed the president about the meeting. "Clinton told Gore," Branch writes, "that he was disappointed that he wasn't used more in the campaign's final days, and that Gore had not developed any overarching theme. Gore countered that Clinton had never personally apologized to him for the Monica Lewinsky scandal… Gore also suggested that Clinton was to blame for his defeat by George W. Bush.

'I thought he was in Neverland', Clinton told Branch."[ccxxvi]

In reading the Clinton memoir, *My Life*, it is hard to find an acknowledgment that this tension even existed. It reads like Clinton was an active participant in helping the Gore campaign and avoids any mention of difficulties between the two men.

Gore, in one of his first interviews since the election, told Barbara Walters that "he does not believe Bill Clinton's sexual indiscretions contributed to his defeat, telling Walters that voters were plenty smart enough to distinguish between his [Clinton's] personal life and his accomplishments as president." He acknowledged that he and Clinton had a stormy meeting in December 2000 over campaign strategy. "I wanted to clear the air," Gore told Walters, adding that "it worked and that he and Clinton remain comrades in arms."[ccxxvii]

Despite these public characterizations by the two principals, many people who knew one or both of them describe the matter quite differently. Michael Takiff wrote a book in 2010 in which he interviewed 171 people about Bill Clinton. Among them were:

- Former Massachusetts Governor Michael Dukakis, the 1988 Democratic nominee for president
- Elaine Kamarck, a White House staff member for four years in the Clinton administration
- Joe Lockhart, former White House press secretary during the Clinton administration
- Historian Douglas Brinkley
- Former Congressman Dave McCurdy (D-OK).

Michael Dukakis: Had Clinton not gotten involved with Monica Lewinsky, Gore would have won by 15 points.

Elaine Kamarck: In the first term Gore and Clinton had a great relationship. During the second term Gore was very angry at Clinton for the Lewinsky thing. So what had been a very strong relationship fell apart.

There's no doubt that it was Clinton's fault. When you look at the exit polls for 2000, Gore's percentage of the vote in the various subgroups was the same as Clinton's from 1996 or better, because he got more Democratic votes than Clinton did in 1996. With the exception of one category of voters…Married women…they vote 6 points less for Gore than they did for Clinton in '96. That was not about environmental policy.

The Republicans were looking for a scandal, but he didn't have to give it to them. That's the bottom line, and until Bill Clinton himself can face that – I mean, come on. Come on. It wasn't the Republicans who had him fooling around with that little girl. He was always reckless. It's his fatal flaw. He's blind when it comes to this, always has been. This was so much the way he behaved that the White House wasn't going to change him, although everybody hoped it would.

Joe Lockhart: Gore found Clinton's behavior abhorrent, but it was more than that. I think Gore for eight years chafed under the idea, "Who is this guy? I'm the guy who should be president." It was fine for the first couple years, then it got a little uncomfortable, then it got very uncomfortable when Clinton sometimes got in the way. Clinton tends to fill the stage.

Douglas Brinkley: Clinton's in total denial about it. It's a misunderstanding of the damage he did.

Dave McCurdy: He accomplished a lot. Unfortunately, the legacy is incomplete because of the personal failings. Al Gore would have won had it not been for Lewinsky. That's a bad legacy.[ccxxviii] Their relationship, which had started off so well, would not be repaired for several years.

A story has circulated around Washington after 9/11 that may or may not be true. When the World Trade Center was attacked, Gore was in Paris watching the TV broadcast with French officials, declaring that Osama bin Laden had to be the guilty party. He immediately began calling former staffers to help him get back to the United States when flights to the U.S. were being canceled. Instead, he arranged to fly to Toronto; a driver would pick him up there and drive him to DC. Bill Clinton, as the story goes, got wind of this and sent a message that he'd like to have his former running mate stop for the night at the new Clinton home in Chappaqua, New York. On arrival, Gore got out of the car as Clinton emerged from his house, still largely under construction. In the front yard was a dumpster and a toilet awaiting its installation.

"I see, you brought a bit of Arkansas to New York," was the Gore quip. With that, the iciness between them began to melt.

Al Gore may reflect on the stubbornness he showed about Clinton's behavior and decide that they should have campaigned together. Losing is hard and it is easy to make an argument that keeping Clinton away led to that loss. Elections matter and the person elected president matters as well.

Would there have been an Iraq war with Al Gore as president? It is impossible to know but it is easy to argue that the Gore campaign decision to keep Bill Clinton at arm's length was a bad decision indeed.

George W. Bush – Courtesy the Library of Congress

George W. Bush – WMD

George W. Bush was the 43rd president of the United States. Elected in 2000 and re-elected in 2004, his presidency was largely successful except for one glaring issue that may be considered a bad mistake – the Iraq war. Not everyone would agree, but it isn't difficult to outline why this policy was a bad one.

Not only were a large number of people killed and wounded, but the premise behind the reason for war was false. The ripple effect from Bush's decision has been felt for decades. It can be argued that a nation should only go to war when it must, when it is the last resort. This war was begun by choice.

The genesis of the conflict goes back to the administration of George H.W. Bush, father of George W. They were the only father-son presidencies since John Adams and son John Quincy Adams nearly two centuries earlier. During the term of the first Bush, the United States led an international coalition to stop the aggression of Iraq's Saddam Hussein when he invaded the nation of Kuwait. It was a brief and overwhelmingly successful military action that ended the Iraqi invasion and occupation. The Bush administration debated whether or not to continue the conflict until Hussein was removed from power. But the decision was made that regime change was not the goal of the United States and if Hussein had been removed, the U.S. responsibility for maintaining peace and stability in Iraq would be tremendous.

The Department of Justice's office of the inspector general issued a report about an assassination attempt by Iraqis aimed at killing President Bush. Bush visited Kuwait after the hostilities ceased and after the end of his presidency. The plot to kill the former president with a car bomb was uncovered by Kuwaiti officials, who arrested 17 men involved in the plot.

Bush had been defeated by Bill Clinton in the 1992 election, and Clinton, during the first six months of his presidency, retaliated in defense of his predecessor. Missiles were launched against the Iraqi Intelligence Service.[ccxxix]

One can only imagine how the eldest son felt upon learning about the threat against his father.

Then came September 11, 2001, barely eight months into the presidency of George W. Bush. Islamic terrorists hijacked four American commercial jets, crashing two into the twin towers of the World Trade Center in New York City. The third crashed into the Pentagon and a fourth in Pennsylvania, due to the insurrection mounted by passengers against the terrorists. Its goal was likely the U.S. Capitol or the White House. Nearly 3,000 Americans died that day along with scores who were injured. The pain of that dreadful day is still felt in America to this day.

The United States had been fairly immune to international terrorism prior to 9/11. The events of that day inaugurated a war on terrorism that would become the centerpiece of the Bush presidency.

The entire nation looked to President Bush to retaliate against those who attacked America. The country was traumatized, and it became clear right away that action would be taken against those responsible. President Bush announced the *War on Terror* within days, a war that has continued ever since. The intelligence community knew immediately that the attacks had been orchestrated by a terror organization known as Al-Qaeda, led by a wealthy Saudi Arabian, Osama bin Laden. He had been supported by the Taliban leaders in Afghanistan.

The president was presented with three options by his political and military leadership, his war council. The first was to bomb Al-Qaeda camps in Afghanistan with targeted missile strikes. The second was to add manned bombers to the attacking force, widening the area to be struck. Option three was to add boots on the ground, American armed forces. During the discussion, the focus shifted to Iraq and the brutal dictatorship of Saddam Hussein, long thought to be a supporter of anti-American terrorists. In Bush's memoir, he described the Iraqi regime as "widely considered the most dangerous country in the world."

Defense Secretary Donald Rumsfeld was quoted as saying, "Dealing with Iraq would show a major commitment to anti-terrorism."

Secretary of State Colin Powell counseled against it. "Going after Iraq now would be viewed as a bait and switch...We would lose the UN, the Islamic countries, and NATO. If we want to do Iraq, we should do it at a time of our choosing. But we should not do it now, because we don't have linkage to this event."

His view was seconded by CIA Director George Tenet, adding that the "first target needs to be al Qaeda."

Vice President Richard Cheney concurred with the view that the Hussein threat had to be addressed but, "now is not a good time to do it."[ccxxx]

While the attacks against Afghanistan were taking place, less than a month after 9/11, letters containing the highly toxic anthrax were received in the offices of major news outlets as well as the United States Senate. At least five deaths were reported from the anthrax, and fears of a biological attack on the country were growing.

Leaders in the Bush administration tried to institute procedures to protect the public from anthrax delivered through the mails while also trying to figure out where the attacks came from. Attention shifted to Iraq, a country with a reputation for using weapons of mass destruction (WMD) and which had publicly acknowledged possession of anthrax in 1995.

Al-Qaeda was also suspected but there was no evidence that either source was responsible. It would be nine years before the justice department would determine that an American government scientist had sent the poisonous letters.[ccxxxi]

In less than six months after the attacks of 9/11, the Taliban was removed from power in Afghanistan by the American military, the Al-Qaeda camps were destroyed, and the foundations for a democratic government were established. But it also became clear that the stability then being enjoyed in Afghanistan could only be maintained by the presence of substantial U.S. armed forces.

The liberation of Afghanistan had cost 27 American lives at its conclusion, but American losses would continue and grow as Taliban resistance persisted. Over the next two decades, armed attacks occurred with more American losses in each succeeding year. The young democracy could only be maintained by the American military presence that existed for the remainder of the Bush presidency.

That presence was maintained and increased with consistent instability in the country through the administrations of Barack Obama and Donald Trump, ending only when President Joe Biden removed American troops. The government immediately fell, and the Taliban was returned to power.

As the war on Afghanistan during the Bush presidency became less of a priority, attention shifted to the perceived threat from Iraq. Saddam Hussein was assumed to be amassing increased numbers of weapons of mass destruction including biological agents. Throughout 2002, Bush rallied an international coalition to demand the end of the Iraqi WMD program. In early 2002, at his State of the Union message, Bush labeled Iraq as part of an *Axis of Evil*.

Congress authorized the military action against Iraq in October 2002. United Nations Security Council resolutions were passed requiring Iraq to come clean about its inventory of WMD, threatening severe consequences for continued defiance. And that defiance did continue. Negotiations with Iraq had failed. Threats from the international coalition were ignored. By March 2003, the decision to execute Operation Iraqi Freedom was made.

According to the American General Tommy Franks, overall commander in the war, there were eight objectives of the invasion: "First, ending the regime of Saddam Hussein. Second, to identify, isolate, and eliminate Iraq's weapons of mass destruction. Third, to search for, to capture, and to drive out terrorists from that country. Fourth, to collect such intelligence as we can relate to terrorist networks. Fifth, to collect such intelligence as we can relate to the global network of illicit weapons of mass destruction. Sixth, to end sanctions and to immediately deliver humanitarian support to the displaced and to many needy Iraqi citizens. Seventh, to secure Iraq's oil fields and resources, which belong to the Iraqi people. And last, to help the Iraqi people create conditions for a transition to representative self-government."[ccxxxii]

President Bush, in his memoir, summarized his reasons for attacking Saddam Hussein. First, he described Hussein as "waging a low-grade war against the United States" from early 2001 and had fired at our pilots patrolling the no-fly zones seven hundred times. After the terrorist attacks on 9/11, he turned his attention to Hussein. Assessing those states considered to be sponsors of terror, he saw them as sworn enemies of the U.S. They threatened their neighbors, violated the demands of the international community, repressed their own people, and pursued WMD.

His conclusion was that Iraq "combined all those threats."

He went on to describe Saddam Hussein in several ways. Hussein didn't just sympathize with terrorists, he supported them. He had shown his hatred of America by firing on our pilots and trying to kill Bush's father. His threats to his neighbors included actual invasions, Iran in the 1980s, and Kuwait in the 1990s. His brutality included the torture of innocent people, rapes of political opponents, beheadings, and other mass atrocities.

He had used WMD against Iran, specifically mustard gas and nerve agents, giving the president reasons to assume those weapons were still in his possession. If Hussein couldn't prove that he no longer had WMD, his removal was justified. Despite that justification, the world would be better off without Saddam Hussein, something of which few people disagreed.[ccxxxiii]

Bush wrote about intelligence reports he had received that Hussein had enhanced "the infrastructure and expertise necessary for WMD production." He was advised that Iraq was "almost certainly working to produce the causative agent for anthrax along with botulinum toxin, aflatoxin, and ricin." He felt that Hussein's history taught us that he produced these weapons not to deter but in order to use them.[ccxxxiv]

But Bush went further, explaining in his memoir that he and British Prime Minister Tony Blair agreed that once Hussein was removed, they would be obligated to replace his regime with a democratic government.[ccxxxv]

Airstrikes began in Baghdad, the Iraqi capital, on March 19. The hostilities would end only if Hussein destroyed his WMD and the international community was able to verify that destruction. Hussein's defiance continued as did the airstrikes.

Not long after the bombing had begun, American ground forces were introduced, and the Iraqi army quickly gave way. The Ba'athist government collapsed, and eventually, Saddam Hussein was captured and later executed.

American military personnel were instructed to find the WMD and any existing biological weapons. To the surprise and consternation of the administration, none were found. The Bush administration had consistently stated that these weapons existed but was never able to provide concrete evidence. The insistence of respected officials like General Colin Powell, then secretary of state, convinced Congress and the American public that the WMD existed, despite the lack of hard evidence.

In late 2002, Congress authorized, and President Bush signed into law, the creation of a commission to study the circumstances leading to the 9/11 attack, The National Commission on Terrorist Attacks upon the United States, later known as the 9/11 Commission. It was chaired by former New Jersey Governor Thomas Kean and former Indiana Congressman Lee Hamilton.

This bi-partisan commission determined that the attacks took place because of the failures of the American intelligence community, specifically the CIA and FBI. But it also concluded that there were no WMD in Iraq, no biological weapons, and no evidence of any relationship between Saddam Hussein and Al-Qaeda. In other words, the justification for the war was in error; it did not exist.

While American officials were dismayed that no WMD were found, they shouldn't have been surprised. In November 2002, the United Nations issued Resolution 1441. It set up a process for inspections within Iraq and was accepted by Saddam Hussein.

The chair of the UN Monitoring, Verification and Inspection Commission (UNMOVIC), Hans Blix, and the director general of the International Atomic Energy Agency (IAEA), Mohamed El Baradei, reported in February 2003 that they "found no evidence or plausible indication of the revival of a nuclear weapons program in Iraq...certain items which could have been used in nuclear enrichment centrifuges, such as aluminum tubes, were in fact intended for other uses." In March 2003, Blix said, progress had been made in inspections, and no evidence of WMD had been found. [ccxxxvi]

The conflict with Iraq, despite its justification being in error, continued throughout the remainder of the Bush presidency. American armed forces ranged in size from a low of 192,000 to as many as 466,000 at its height. Other countries contributed forces as well with the United Kingdom sending 45,000 members of its armed forces into the conflict.

Other participating nations sent far fewer, making the war principally an American one. Deaths in Iraq, both military and civilian, have been estimated to exceed 1.2 million according to ORB International, an independent polling agency located in London. It internally displaced an estimated 3.3 million Iraqis.

The secretary-general of the United Nations, Kofi Annan, called the invasion illegal under international law and in violation of the UN Charter. [ccxxxvii] In 2016, the British Chilcot Report concluded that the United Kingdom had not considered every peaceful solution prior to war. It considered the decision to go to war as *far from satisfactory*.

It pointed out the errors in fact-finding relative to the WMD and asserted that Saddam Hussein was not an imminent threat. Then Prime Minister Tony

Blair assured President Bush that he would be with him *whatever*.[ccxxxviii] Blair's popularity fell during the Iraq conflict, leading to his resignation in 2007.

It was the hope of President Bush that Iraq could be turned into a stable democracy and multi-party elections were held in 2005. The religious tensions so common in the Middle East existed in full force in Iraq. Its Sunni minority had been dominant prior to the elections and became alienated by the policies enacted after the election.

A September 2002 report by Major General Glen Shaffer discussed the conclusions of the Joint Chiefs of Staff that the Iraqi WMD program was considerably less advanced than had been publicly stated. The intelligence was considered imprecise, and its conclusions were based more on analytic assumptions than hard evidence.[ccxxxix]

Former President Bill Clinton also weighed in when addressing a Labour Party conference in England. "As a preemptive action today, however well-justified, may come back with unwelcome consequences in the future...I don't care how precise your bombs and your weapons are when you set them off, innocent people will die."[ccxl]

Congress had provided President Bush with what he needed to make war but there were severe divisions in both houses. In the House of Representatives, more than half of the Democrats opposed the authorization. Twenty-one of the 50 Democratic senators also voted no. Cautions were expressed that there was no exit strategy, that America would own Iraq, and that we should do more to prevent an armed conflict. Similar voices in opposition were heard in England's House of Commons.

Pope John Paul II publicly condemned the military intervention, which was also expressed privately to the president. Other world leaders also spoke out in opposition, including Nelson Mandela, France's foreign minister, and Germany's foreign secretary.

On May 1, 2003, President Bush declared "Mission Accomplished," from the aircraft carrier USS Abraham Lincoln. But America's role in Iraq was far from complete. The Iraqi interim government was declared in charge after the United States signed over sovereignty in June 2004. Serious fighting, however, had been taking place throughout this period.

Americans were horrified by scenes of American contractors who were killed and their bodies dragged through the streets. The effort to pacify the city resulted in the First Battle of Fallujah in April 2004 with the bloodiest battle of the war fought only seven months later in the Second Battle of Fallujah.

Also in 2004, Americans were horrified to see press reports of prisoner abuse at Abu Ghraib with American soldiers taunting and abusing Iraqi prisoners. Americans and Iraqis continued to die over the next several months from thousands of insurgent attacks, suicide bombers, and the wide use of IEDs, improvised explosive devices.

In late 2006, former Secretary of State James Baker and former Indiana Congressman Lee Hamilton co-chaired the Iraq Study Group. They released a report saying, "the situation in Iraq is grave and deteriorating" and "US forces seem to be caught in a mission that has no foreseeable end." The report's 79 recommendations include increasing diplomatic measures with *Iran and Syria,* and intensifying efforts to train Iraqi troops. That same month the Pentagon reported that insurgent attacks were averaging about 960 attacks per week, the highest since the reports had begun in 2005.[ccxli]

In 2007, President Bush announced what would become known as a *surge*. More American armed forces would be sent to Iraq to try and quell the violence and bring the long-hoped-for stability. Months later, the Iraqi government would call on the United States to set a timetable for withdrawal. Coalition forces would begin to withdraw, adding new pressures on the American military. American leaders would soon start promising similar withdrawals of troops.

The surge, however, seemed to be having its intended effect by early 2008. Violence in Iraq had declined substantially. The United States announced its intention to withdraw armed forces from Iraq by June 2009. For many Iraqis, this was not sufficient as President Bush's effigy was burned in a central Baghdad square. But as the world looked toward the finality of the war, George Bush would no longer be president. Barack Obama was elected in November 2008 and Iraq would be among his problems to solve.

President Obama, early in his presidency, announced a continuation of American withdrawal from Iraq. As the troops began leaving in stages, a new phenomenon threatened the stability in Iraq. The Islamic State, or ISIL (also ISIS), rose throughout the country, and the number of terrorist attacks began to rise. Fighting ISIL became the new American priority.

With continued sectarian conflict, insurgent attacks, and ISIL atrocities, American focus on Iraq had to continue. The final withdrawal of American troops would not end until the final days of 2011. It wouldn't be until 2018 that ISIL would be defeated; Iraq would reach its lowest level of violence in a decade.

According to the U.S. Department of Defense casualty website, there were 4,431 total American deaths and 31,994 wounded in action as a result of the Iraq war. The total cost of the war was estimated to be $1.7 trillion by the Watson Institute for International and Public Affairs at Brown University.[ccxlii] The losses in Iraq were far greater, human losses as well as economic and severe ecological damage. The effect on American prestige is incalculable.

The United States has always prided itself on being able to assume the moral high ground. The Iraq war makes that more difficult. From the erroneous basis for the decision to invade to the destruction in Iraq to the American abuses of Iraqi prisoners to the damage within American alliances to the rise of terrorism, there are many ways to justify strong criticisms of George Bush's decision.

While Bush described the war to be central to his War on Terror, it can be argued that the war actually increased terrorism. The invasion and continued occupation of Iraq served as a recruiting agent for future terrorists. A counter-terrorism expert, Rohan Gunaratna, referred to the invasion of Iraq as a fatal mistake.[ccxliii]

The journalist Steve Coll has written about Saddam Hussein, specifically addressing the reasons why Hussein hid the fact that there were no WMDs. He had found them necessary in the 1980s in order to deter Iran and Israel but destroyed much of his arsenal in 1991. He maintained the illusion that he still had them to ensure he would stay in power after his humiliating defeat by the United States when he was evicted from Kuwait under the first President Bush.

His problems were made more acute by his inability to account for where the weapons had gone. Also, he had had an inconsistent history with the United States. The Reagan administration had cultivated him, seeing him as a bulwark against Iran, and turned a blind eye away from Hussein's use of chemical weapons against his own people.

After the first Iraq war, regime change became the policy of the subsequent Clinton and Bush administrations, but Hussein misinterpreted the seriousness of the American intent. Coll also debunks the story about the attempted assassination of George H.W. Bush, one of the motivations behind George W.

Bush's desire to remove the Iraqi leader. There were clearly miscalculations on both sides.[ccxliv]

On the 20th anniversary of the invasion, the Council on Foreign Relations released a report on the rationale for going to war and the subsequent decisions during the occupation. The report states that the "justification for going to war was based on scanty and deeply flawed intelligence" and that the invasion was an "error compounded by the absence of an agreed exit strategy and the decision to embark on a massive, open-ended nation-building project...the occupation authority's first acts were to disband the Iraqi army and the Ba'athist governing party, igniting what would become a lethal, long-running insurgency and eventually a multinational terrorist organization that took over most of the country." Also in this report was this: "The costs of the Iraq War have been calculated at *$8 trillion* if the veterans' healthcare costs are included; some *300,000 Iraqi civilians* were killed, over *9 million displaced*, and *4,598 U.S. troops and 3,650 contractors* were killed."[ccxlv]

Had Iraq become the democratic island of stability in the most unstable region of the world, it might be better argued that the decision to invade was justified. That is hardly the case, however, and the costs of this decision were very high. The Stockholm International Peace Research Institute (SIPRI) described the status of Iraq in 2023:

"Today Iraq is enjoying its most stable period since 2003. Armed violence persists in different forms, but it is sporadic, fragmented, and localized. However, the country remains fragile and divided, and its people face an array of deepening challenges that the state is struggling to address."[ccxlvi]

History will better judge whether it was justified as President Bush felt or whether it was not.

John Kerry – Courtesy the Library of Congress

John Kerry – Swift Boat

John Kerry first came to the public's attention in April 1971 when he testified before a U.S. Senate Committee against the war in Vietnam.

Wearing his military khakis, good-looking, serious, eloquent, the Vietnam veteran memorably asked the committee, "How do you ask a man to be the last man to die in Vietnam? How do you ask a man to be the last man to die for a mistake?"

Representing the organization Vietnam Veterans Against the War, he described those aspects of the veterans' experiences both fighting in the war and the ways they were received at home upon return. It was his view that government policy was the cause of the war crimes of which he also spoke.

His speech highlighted atrocities, of which those in charge turned a blind eye, of the post-traumatic stresses shared by so many of his fellow veterans, and of the anger and betrayal he felt because of the entire experience. He discussed the difficulty so many of them had in trying to understand why they were in Vietnam at all.

Those patriotic young men going off to *fight for their country* were often badly changed by the experience, if not while serving in Vietnam then by the negative manner in which they were treated by their own countrymen after returning home.

He decried the destruction brought to the Vietnamese, quoting the infamous line that we had to destroy the village in order to save it, with the overall realization that we were not winning. An entire generation of young people, both civilians at home and soldiers abroad were being damaged by the Vietnam saga.[ccxlvii]

Born in 1943 to a military family, he grew up in Massachusetts and Washington, DC, attended boarding schools in New England, and graduated from Yale University. Enlisting in the U.S. Naval Reserve, he attained the rank of lieutenant and served in Vietnam as a naval officer. There he commanded a fast patrol craft known as a Swift Boat. During that time, he was wounded in combat and awarded three Purple Hearts. He was also awarded a Silver Star and Bronze Star for valorous conduct in separate military engagements.

Kerry entered politics the next year, seeking a seat in Congress from Massachusetts. He won the Democratic nomination but lost in the general election. From there, he went to law school and earned his law degree, after which he served as an assistant district attorney in Middlesex County, Massachusetts.

In 1982, he was elected lieutenant governor of Massachusetts, joining the ticket with Michael Dukakis, who would be the Democratic nominee for president in 1988. Kerry would be elected to the U.S. Senate in 1984. Twenty years later, he would be the Democratic nominee for president, seeking to unseat the incumbent, George W. Bush.

He should have won that election. President Bush was elected in 2000 while losing the popular vote to Vice President Al Gore. The Supreme Court halted the recount in the pivotal state of Florida while Bush was slightly ahead, giving him the Electoral College win and the presidency.

The Iraq war, begun after the trauma of the terrorist attacks on September 11, 2001, was still fairly popular but there were significant undercurrents felt in the electorate because of 9/11 and the war. Polling showed that 44% of the public felt terrorism, the Iraq war, and national security to be among the most serious issues.

These heightened concerns made Kerry look good, given his military background. Issues were raised in the campaign, on the other hand, on whether Bush had properly fulfilled his responsibilities in the National Guard many years earlier.

The public also responded poorly to the question of whether the country was on the right track or the wrong track with a majority feeling the latter. The economy, always a central issue, in most elections, was also a problem for Bush. Sixty percent of the voters felt the economy was in bad shape.[ccxlviii]

"I'm John Kerry and I'm reporting for duty," were the words used by John Kerry when introduced to the Democratic National Convention in July 2004. His history as a veteran became the centerpiece of his campaign. It would be the rare campaign indeed in which mistakes aren't made, and Kerry made his share. His own words were used against him by the Bush campaign.

George W. Bush assessed John Kerry when he became the presumptive Democratic nominee for president in 2004. The assets were clear; Vietnam vet, four-term senator, polished debater. But he also zoned in on Kerry's liberal voting record and inconsistencies in his votes and statements.

In 2003, after opposing an appropriations bill to fund troops in Iran and Afghanistan, Kerry was quoted as saying, "I actually did vote for the $87 billion before I voted against it."

Bush told his advisor Karl Rove, shortly after learning this, "The American people expect their president to take a clear stand and defend it, especially, when it comes to supporting troops in combat." This *flip-flop* theme became the centerpiece of ads produced by the Bush campaign.[ccxlix]

During the campaign, Kerry didn't help himself by being photographed windsurfing, hardly a sport that related to the average American. But his biggest mistake was the way he failed to adequately respond to the Swift Boat Veterans for Truth Campaign.

The political action group was comprised of 275 Vietnam veterans who were joined in their opposition to John Kerry's presidential bid. He was charged by them in a series of television ads of "being unfit to lead America as its commander-in-chief." They called into question his "war record, the medals he had been awarded, and even his patriotism. The attacks were direct, personal, and highly effective." From May to October 2004, they raised $6.7 million, spending all but $800,000 of it on the production and airing of those television advertisements. Each ad featured a veteran who described Kerry as "not been honest," "lied," "lying," "dishonored," "cannot be trusted," and "betrayed."

The claims of the organization were largely refuted or debunked by most major news outlets. Several of the featured spokesmen had actually served with Kerry. It seemed that the leaders of the group were motivated mainly by politics and that they had objected to Kerry ever since he made his first public statement against the war.

They may have been legitimately offended by the way he described the experiences that they shared. Nonetheless, the inflammatory ads were not only viewed by large numbers of Americans but they were often replayed at least in part on the evening news shows.[ccl]

One of the leading consultants behind the creation of the TV ads was Chris LaCivita. He would earn greater renown in 2024 as he played a major role in the Donald Trump 2024 presidential campaign.

On August 5, 2004, the Swift Boat Veterans for Truth ads hit the airwaves and were accompanied by many news reports. They generated an amazing amount of free media.

As the chair of the Democratic National Committee Terry McAuliffe wrote, "the Kerry campaign defended itself when the ads first hit, but immediately backed off, hoping the storm would pass. Their argument was that the Swift Boat folks were only putting up a $300,000 ad buy and if you commented, that only generated more attention. They hoped it would go away but it didn't – and the damage it did to Kerry's standing in the polls gave Bush the opening he needed." He goes on to describe comments made at a conference by Bush's media advisor, Mark McKinnon, who said the $300,000 "ad buy was worth $30 million in free media...the Bush campaign was shocked and amazed that the Kerry campaign just sat there and took it. They were also overjoyed."[ccli]

Kerry published a memoir in 2018 that addressed the chain of events and his reactions in detail.

The words in the ad were stark. "John Kerry has not been honest about what happened in Vietnam." "He is lying about his record." "I know John Kerry is lying about his Purple Heart because I treated him for that injury." "John Kerry lied to get his Bronze Star... I know, I was there, I saw what happened." "John Kerry has not been honest." "John Kerry is no war hero." "John Kerry betrayed the men and women he served with in Vietnam."

All of this was hard enough to hear and rebut, but the floodgates opened when a book appeared to accompany the ad, authored by none other than John O'Neill, an operative from 1971, whom Chuck Colson and the Nixon White House recruited to debate the VVAW, and Jerome Corsi, a conspiracy theorist who would later go on to accuse Hillary Clinton of being a lesbian and Barack Obama of being a closeted Muslim. We heard that the book, published by a conservative imprint and leveraged by the right-wing network, would debut at number one on the New York Times bestseller list.

Money, lies, and television – and more money – are a toxic combination.

As our bus rumbled through the countryside, we sensed a new danger building. Our opponents had created an entirely new medium – dozens of outright lies, adding up to one big lie, all footnoted and backed by signed affidavits to strike the pose of being meticulously researched.

I remember standing with our press secretary behind the reception desk at a tiny motel. Page by page, a faxed version of the book, titled Unfit for Command, was coming in to us.

I'd pull each page off the fax machine before it cascaded into the paper tray. The book was filled with lies. The primary author, John O'Neill, implied to have known me from Swift boats; in fact, he had appeared on the scene long after I'd left. Nothing about his reappearance was a coincidence.

People who weren't there were polluting the airwaves with lies, trying to undermine the service of every one of us who was. I was seething. I called my campaign manager. She believed that the advertising buy was minimal, but we were tracking it. John Edwards said the Republicans were just trying to get us to "chase a rabbit."

None of this reassured me. I had lived through too much during the Nixon years to forget what Mark Twain said: "A lie can make it halfway around the world before the truth pulls its boots on." But the campaign made sure the truth started to kick back.

He goes on to describe the manner in which the ads were being debunked and after each example, he follows with, "And yet the ads stayed on the air." At the time, it appeared that the large numbers of newspaper reports were neutralizing the smears but fighting broadcast television with print media is akin to fighting a tank with a BB gun. His instinct was to fight back on TV but was consistently told that they couldn't afford to put up ads at that time; there wouldn't be money enough for ads in October.

One night, in a hotel, late in the campaign, I couldn't sleep. We were in Ohio, and I was restless. I turned on the television and there was the Swift boat ad blatantly lying about me. If I were a citizen watching that ad, if that was my principal frame of reference, I wouldn't vote for me.

He knew the ads were having an impact and argued with his staff, who insisted he defer to the professionals working on his behalf.

In the end, when I look back, I have no one to get mad at but myself – and I've kicked myself many times. It was my campaign. These experts gave me their best judgment as to what they thought I should do. In the final analysis, it was my decision – no one else's – to overrule them or not.

What I should have done was stop the campaign, stand up with my crew and answer every lie in detail and create and air ads to run in every market where theirs ran.

He expresses some ambivalence about his feelings and quotes Ted Kennedy's saying that "if you're explaining, you're losing." But he adds:

It turns out that sometimes you can lose by not explaining, and sometimes, like it or not, you have to address something that's too big and too important to become just another firefight between campaigns.[cclii]

Kerry's initial instincts were good ones and should have carried the day. He knew that these ads were challenging the very core of who he was, as a veteran, as a candidate, and as a man. Yet he was persuaded by his campaign advisors that responding immediately was a mistake. First, their strategy was not to air TV ads until after the Republican Convention in August. Second, early polling showed no impact from the Swift Boat ads. Third, the Swift Boat ad buy was small, and an aggressive response would only generate more attention.

171

There is an old adage in politics that the more you stir manure, the more it smells. Therefore, they decided not to stir the manure. Not long afterward, the polls began showing a very different impact of the ads.

David Remnick, in his book *The Bridge: The Life and Rise of Barack Obama*, said, "John Kerry's inability to rebuff the smears on his character and his record – particularly the attacks on his war record by the well-funded group called the Swift Boat Veterans for Truth – had cost him dearly."[ccliii]

Voters had to wonder, after seeing or hearing about the ads, why Kerry didn't defend himself from such a vitriolic manner of accusations. The campaign remained close; polling continued to show the candidates neck and neck. Bush benefited from the work of Karl Rove, a principal advisor to his campaign, in their advanced level of targeting and voter profiling.

A look back at the two campaigns shows that, at least, as far as campaign technology goes, the Republicans did quite better than the Democrats. But the result was a narrow Bush victory, 2.4% over Kerry in the popular vote. Had Kerry won Ohio, which he lost by just over 2%, he would have won the Electoral College vote.

A Kerry victory would have had a ripple effect on the subsequent years in the United States. That is probably true about any election that may have turned out differently. One example would focus on his running mate, North Carolina Senator John Edwards. Four years after the 2004 election, Edwards was a candidate for the Democratic presidential nomination.

After losing that battle, news stories erupted that John Edwards was not only unfaithful to his wife, then dying of cancer, but had fathered a child out of wedlock. Trying to cover it up, he was later charged with illegally using campaign funds in that effort. The charges were ultimately dismissed but his political career was over. Would these events have taken place had he been elected vice president in 2004? There is no way to know.

Had Kerry been elected in 2004, it is unlikely that Barack Obama would have been elected president in 2008, much less nominated by his party. It is more likely that Kerry would have been seeking re-election and Obama would have remained a senator. The futures of Hillary Clinton, Joseph Biden, John McCain, and Donald Trump would likely have been affected by this change in history.

Each subsequent presidential election would have been different had John Kerry effectively combated the charges of the Swift Boat Veterans for Truth.

His decision not to do so determined the outcome of the 2004 presidential election.

One of the donors to the Swift Boat ads was Texas oilman T. Boone Pickens. Pickens contributed $3 million to the campaign. Three years after that election, in 2007, Pickens offered to pay a million dollars to anyone who could disprove the ads.

Kerry loudly accepted the challenge and offered to meet in public with Pickens to disprove the contents of the negative advertising. Pickens responded with a series of requests for documentation that Kerry seemed unable to provide. A back-and-forth between the men took place without resolution.

Whatever the case, true or not, the charges in the ads made a critical difference in the campaign and in American history since.

Kerry conceded after his election defeat "that his lackluster response likely cost him the election."[ccliv]

John McCain and Sarah Palin – Courtesy of the Carol M. Highsmith Archive collection at the Library of Congress

John McCain – Soccer Mom

U.S. Senator John McCain was the Republican nominee for president in 2008. His choice for a running mate was the little-known Alaska governor and former mayor of Wasilla, Alaska, Sarah Palin. Whether this decision was a good one or a bad one, for McCain and for the country, largely depends on one's feelings about the nature of politics in the third decade of the 21st century.

National politics has been dominated by the extreme left and the extreme right and a political divide that seems intractable, with a Congress that no longer functions well. Increasingly, political adversaries are seen as the enemy and bipartisanship appears outdated and obsolete. The level of civility in the halls of Congress has shrunk to an all-time low.

Most prominent in this divisive era stood Donald J. Trump. Elected president in 2016, he was twice impeached and, after losing the 2020 election and persisting in the argument that the election was stolen, has provided a level of toxicity in American life unknown since the Civil War. In 2024, he was elected president again.

National politics seemed to pivot in this toxic direction with the introduction of Sarah Palin to the public's attention. While this decision may not have affected the likelihood of McCain/Palin being elected in the short term, it represented an event that has changed America in the long term.

How did this choice of a vice-presidential running mate affect the nature of American politics? It's instructive to explore why this decision was made and its impact on the country.

John McCain was born in 1936, the son and grandson of Navy admirals. Being raised in that military family led him to launch his own career as a naval aviator after graduating from the U.S. Naval Academy at the bottom of his class. He was popular, raucous, a ladies' man, and his standing in his class was more a reflection of his behavior than intelligence. He would spend 22 years in the Navy.

His true character was demonstrated after he was shot down over Hanoi in 1967 during the Vietnam War. Imprisoned by the North Vietnamese, beaten and tortured mercilessly for over five years, his captors offered him a release because of his father's status. McCain refused any special treatment and remained in prison until he was part of a general prisoner release in 1973.

McCain achieved a level of fame when arriving in the U.S. with the other prisoners and being televised while President Richard Nixon greeted them. After a considerable time dealing with his injuries, he remained in the Navy and eventually became the Navy's liaison to the U.S. Senate.

Working in and around Congress sparked an interest in politics that he had not felt previously. He retired from the Navy, moved to Arizona, and in 1982, he was a successful candidate for the U.S. House of Representatives.

He served ably as a strong supporter of then President Ronald Reagan. When the Arizona icon, long-time Senator Barry Goldwater, announced his retirement in 1986, McCain shifted his attention and was successfully elected to the Senate.

He became embroiled in a scandal when named one of the Keating Five, having accepted contributions and gifts from Charles Keating, whose bank was being seized by the federal government because of various banking violations. The subsequent Senate investigation showed McCain to have acted unwisely in a manner that appeared improper, but he was cleared of any actual illegality. Nonetheless, the scandal didn't prevent his re-election in 1992.

During the ensuing years, he earned a reputation for being a maverick, someone who voted his conscience and not always as his party would wish. He saw himself as someone "with a strong moral compass who was willing to buck his party and admit when he was wrong." [cclv]

He opposed military actions in Somalia during the Clinton presidency, supported Clinton's Supreme Court nominations, sponsored campaign finance reform, and took on the tobacco industry in a number of ways. Considered a few times for the vice presidency, during the George H.W. Bush campaign in 1988 and again with Sen. Bob Dole in 1996, McCain decided to seek the presidency himself in 2000.

McCain found himself running for the nomination against Texas governor and presidential son, George W. Bush. In a famously dirty campaign, in which McCain accused the Bush campaign of scurrilous tactics and lies, Bush won the nomination and McCain returned to the Senate. After Bush's two terms, McCain decided to try again.

The 2008 election would be the first time since 1952 that neither the incumbent president nor vice president sought the presidency. McCain entered the race as a well-known candidate to Republican voters, but the early front-runner was former New York City Mayor Rudolph Giuliani. Other contenders for the nomination were former Tennessee Senator Fred Thompson, Arkansas Governor Mike Huckabee, former Massachusetts Governor Mitt Romney, and Texas Representative Ron Paul. McCain prevailed over all of them in the early primaries and was the presumptive Republican nominee by the end of February.

The Democrats also fielded a large number of candidates including former first lady and current New York Senator Hillary Clinton, the 2000 vice-presidential nominee, North Carolina Senator John Edwards, Delaware Senator Joe Biden, New Mexico Governor Bill Richardson, Iowa Governor Tom Vilsack, and Indiana Senator Evan Bayh.

But it was the entry of Illinois Senator Barack Obama that changed the race and quickly turned it into a two-candidate contest between him and Clinton. Obama had surged to public renown because of the speech he gave at the 2004 Democratic Convention and as an eloquent African American politician.

He prevailed over Clinton to win the nomination and for the first time ever, both parties would have United States senators as their standard bearers. Only two sitting senators had ever been elected president throughout American history, Warren Harding and John Kennedy.

McCain's disadvantages were his age – he'd turn 72 during the campaign – and the unpopularity of the incumbent Republican president, George W. Bush. Later in the year, the major disadvantage would be an economic crisis that threatened the country with another great depression. But he also represented experience over the young and relatively inexperienced Obama.

One of McCain's closest friends was the Democratic senator from Connecticut and the 2000 standard-bearer of his party for vice president, Joseph Lieberman. McCain seriously considered adding Lieberman to his ticket, making it the first time a bi-partisan ticket would be presented to the country. It also fit with his maverick image that he valued.

But Lieberman's positions on a woman's right to choose, gun control, and other issues unpopular with rank-and-file Republicans scuttled the idea. It would have been a *Hail Mary* that might have made the Republican ticket more successful but was not to be. Instead, McCain chose another candidate that he saw as a *Hail Mary*, Sarah Palin.

In the Public Television (PBS) series of episodes in September and October 2016 called "The Contenders: 16 for 16," a contrast was shown between the two female nominees for vice president, Geraldine Ferraro in 1984 and Sarah Palin in 2008. Both were, in a way, a choice likened to a *Hail Mary*, in that something was required to shake up each race in order to have a chance at turning the prospects around. As Ronald Reagan faced a second term in 1984, the U.S. had just come out of the deep recession in 1981–82, the economy was booming, high-tech innovations were dominating the news, and the country had just experienced the successful Los Angeles Olympics. Reagan was very popular and riding a wave.

Former Vice President Walter Mondale, who had entered the race prior to this wave, won the nomination after a spirited contest with Colorado Senator Gary Hart. By the time he began thinking about a running mate, it was clear that something out of the norm was necessary. "I was trying to come up with something more dramatic," said Mondale.

Congresswoman Geraldine Ferraro had been a teacher and a New York prosecutor prior to her election to Congress. She had obvious qualifications as a possible choice to be the first woman nominated for national office by a major party. Women's groups had grown far stronger in American politics than ever before. Their voices were loudly urging Mondale to choose a woman for his running mate and even House Speaker Tip O'Neill recommended Ferraro. She was one of only 24 women in Congress at the time, and her qualifications seemed to set her apart from her peers. Mondale chose her and she was formally nominated at the Democratic Convention in San Francisco on July 19, 1984.

While her choice gave the Democratic ticket renewed energy and a substantial bump in the polls, the downsides of her nomination began to become clear very soon after leaving San Francisco. First, she was totally new to national press attention, which created significant challenges for her. Second, she was a pro-choice Catholic and started encountering criticism from Catholic leaders and pro-life activists practically immediately.

Her immediate stumbles got worse when she was repeatedly asked about making her taxes public. She replied that she would make hers public but not those of her husband, real estate executive John Zaccaro. To make this news worse, she quoted him, saying, "I won't tell you how to run the country; you don't tell me how to run my business," followed by her comment, "People married to Italian men, you know what it's like."

Reporter Lynn Sherr commented on the program that her remarks turned her into a politician and into a wife, neither of which was what she wanted.

Ultimately, however, voters do not generally vote for the vice president but for the presidential candidates and Reagan defeated Mondale in a landslide, 61–39%. The Ferraro nomination had energized the party but by the time November came around, she was unable to make a major difference in the results of the election.[cclvi]

It would be 24 years before either party tried it again.

The Spectator provided a good summary of the McCain decision. "In 2008, veteran Arizona Senator John McCain was faced with the decision of selecting a running mate. In order to offset his image as an aging, insufficiently conservative Washington insider, he selected Palin, the young conservative outsider. Palin was anti-abortion and pro-oil drilling, and she would be present to appeal to the kinds of strident, outspoken conservatives that had always been wary of the more moderate McCain."[cclvii]

Her candidacy was like red meat to many conservative Republicans. Her charges reflected a belief that elitists ran the country and, with the slanted media, cared nothing for hard-working Americans who came from humble backgrounds.

She ignited a series of culture wars that have continued to this day. For those voters who may have opposed Obama because of his race, she provided a convenient justification for opposing him on the basis that he was an elitist.

The Washington Post described her as the "right-wing, populist governor of Alaska."[cclviii]

Washington Post columnist Dana Milbank titled a piece he wrote about her as, "The Mother of the Trump Movement? You Betcha – It Was Her." He wrote about "how Palin led directly to Trump. Just as Palin couldn't answer NBC reporter Katie Couric's question about what newspapers or magazines she read ('Um, all of them, any of them that have been in front of me all these years'), Trump told *Meet the Press* host Chuck Todd he learned about the military by saying, 'Well, I watch the shows…You know, when you watch your show and all of the other shows'. They shared *'attacks on the media, the demonization of a supposed establishment'.* The huge and sometimes violent crowds. The prominent platforms given both candidates by Fox News. The racist responses among supporters. The paranoia about taking away guns. The suspicion of science. The scapegoating of Muslims. The portrayal of President Obama as something other than an American."[cclix]

David Remnick, in his book *The Bridge: The Life and Rise of Barack Obama*, wrote: "Privately, McCain's aides knew that they had done themselves enormous injury by nominating Sarah Palin. She proved herself so wildly undereducated in the affairs of the country and the world, so willing to say or do anything as long as she attracted attention, that it made McCain look weak and, worse, cynical. Like Rudy Giuliani, she disgraced herself by mocking Obama for working for the poor as a community organizer. It is unclear that another Vice-Presidential nominee would have helped McCain avoid losing – not in the midst of an economic free-fall with a weak, unpopular Republican President in the White House – but she did help him lose ingloriously. She behaved erratically, heedlessly, and McCain did nothing to stop her. By giving himself over to her rhetoric, by failing to put an end to the sort of smears she reveled in, McCain had forfeited some part of what he valued most in himself – his sense of honor."[cclx]

Talking about Sarah Palin, McCain campaign manager Steve Schmidt said that she was "not able to grow beyond her limitations" and went on to characterize the campaign. "Senator John McCain, not your typical Republican candidate in that he took stands contrary to his party's wishes to the point where he was labeled a '*maverick*'. He had competed against George W. Bush for the nomination in 2000 and was defeated in a battle that left him bitter. In 2008, he had reason to be bitter about Bush again as the two-term president was woefully unpopular. To make things worse, the Democratic candidate was Barack Obama, the first African American to win a major party nomination for either national office. He was an elegant, charismatic, incredibly smart candidate with a rousing speaking style. His message of hope was pitted against the McCain message of experience. And McCain knew that hope would beat experience any day in the week."

McCain wanted to shake up Washington and loved his maverick image. And it was clear to him that if he was to have any chance of defeating Obama, he really needed to jolt the campaign, thus a Hail Mary choice very similar to the one Mondale made in 1984. He was interested in learning more about another political figure known as a maverick, the governor of Alaska Sarah Palin.

Palin had been the mayor of her hometown of Wasilla, Alaska, and had shaken up the Alaskan political establishment with her election to the governor's chair. She was great-looking, young, energetic, and rambunctious, articulate with a compelling sense of humor. On paper, she looked good, but she soon showed that she wasn't up to the task.

She was positioned to be the attack dog against Obama, something McCain preferred not to be. But even that role suffered when she showed that she didn't have intellectual heft, and didn't know issues or policy. Her forays into the world of the national press did not go well. When asked about the Bush Doctrine in one interview, she didn't know what it was. *Saturday Night Live* did fabulous parodies of her misstatements. When TV reporter Katie Couric asked her what newspapers or magazines she read, it was clear that she didn't read any. She didn't like and wouldn't take instruction. Sen. Joseph Biden, who was running for vice president on the Democratic ticket, said that dropping her into the vice-presidential race was "a baptism of fire." He added that she had failed the "commander-in-chief test." Schmidt goes on to describe the Palin choice as, "The biggest fucking mistake in my entire life."[cclxi]

The issue for John McCain, however, was that he was choosing someone to stand one heartbeat away from the president, should he be elected. And at the age of 72, he would be the oldest man ever elected to that office at the time. His age and recent bouts with cancer should have made him focus more on her qualifications and ability than he clearly did.

As it turned out, just before the election, the economy collapsed, and America faced the greatest financial crisis since the Great Depression. Even had Sarah Palin been the greatest running mate ever, it wouldn't have made a difference in the election. But John McCain made a decision that, it can be argued, was irresponsible and dangerous to the American people. To many Americans, his choice of Palin disqualified him to be president.

Seeing the Palin choice as an attempt to woo away female supporters of Hillary Clinton, disgruntled because Obama had taken away her opportunity to be president, Gloria Steinem, in her memoir entitled *My Life on the Road*, described the choice of Sarah Palin as "the biggest political mistake since the first President Bush appointed Clarence Thomas to the Supreme Court, expecting to get more votes from African Americans."[cclxii]

Syndicated columnist Kathleen Parker wrote about the choice for a running mate that Biden was considering in July 2020. Looking back at 2008, she wrote, "Back then, the whispered word was that Democrat-turned-Independent Joe Lieberman was McCain's top choice. But the powers that used to be wanted a relatively unknown dynamo from Alaska – then Gov. Sarah Palin. After a chat with McCain in Sedona, Ariz., where all manner of magic is said to occur, the roguish, pro-life mom of five, got a wink and a nod and changed the course of our politics.

With three clicks of her red, shiny shoes, the wonder from Wasilla helped usher the Grand Old Party into a regressive era of ignorance, intransigence, and an ideological muddle of racism, sexism, and nationalistic xenophobia that ultimately produced a Confederate-flag defending, authoritarian-worshipping, Queens-bred reality-TV star named Donald Trump."[cclxiii]

The Spectator wrote about Palin's legacy:

"Palin became a political celebrity in the years after the 2008 campaign, writing books, becoming a TV star with shows on Fox News and TLC, and raising money with her own political action committee SarahPAC. She put these skills to use in the 2010 midterms, becoming a key fixture in the right-wing Tea Party movement and frequently appearing as a keynote speaker at rallies. It was Palin who coined the term 'death panels' to describe the hypothetical rationing of healthcare by bureaucrats under President Obama's healthcare reform. She also criticized Obama for a perceived lack of patriotism. In her book *America By Heart: Reflections on Family, Faith, and Flag*, she expressed her belief that ordinary Americans are tired of Obama's global apology tour and of hearing about what a weak country America is from left-wing professors and journalists."

While these attacks might seem outlandish, they changed conversations within conservative circles and began to affect the political process at large. The hysteria over '*death panels*' helped rally conservatives in 2010 to take back the House and begin their decade-long crusade to repeal the Affordable Care Act. Attacks on Obama's patriotism devolved into the birtherism movement, prominently led by Donald Trump. The moderate politics of John McCain were no more.[cclxiv]

Palin would become an ally of Trump, who famously argued that John McCain was not a hero because he preferred people who were never captured as McCain was. McCain, on the other hand, demonstrated an opposition to

Trump and his style of politics with the most public of examples being the way in which he helped kill Trump's efforts to end the Affordable Care Act from the floor of the United States Senate.

Perhaps, if one has the view that the impact of the Palin choice may have been good for the country, it is instructive to know that as far as John McCain was concerned, he would later say that he regretted the decision.[cclxv] While it may not have affected the outcome of the election, her emergence at the behest of John McCain ushered in an era of politics that has dominated the country since, with ripple effects that may impact the future of all Americans.

Honorable Mentions

There are obviously other unforced errors that could have been highlighted here. Some decisions were bad for the decider but not necessarily for the country and posterity. Other decisions were badly made but turned out to have a positive outcome. Many bad decisions were too minor to be included.

The 15 unforced errors herein affected the political leaders by tarnishing the legacy of the particular leader, determining the future of the particular presidency, or were campaign decisions that led to political defeat. The legacies were tarnished by the decisions of John and John Quincy Adams, Theodore and Franklin Roosevelt, Woodrow Wilson, Richard Nixon, Lyndon Johnson, and George W. Bush.

The future of each presidency was negatively affected by the bad decisions of John Quincy Adams, Thomas Platt, Theodore Roosevelt, Richard Nixon, Lyndon Johnson, and George H.W. Bush. And campaign decisions that didn't go well largely determined the unsuccessful candidacies of Al Gore, John Kerry, and John McCain.

As mentioned at the beginning of this book, the unforced errors to be highlighted should be seriously considered and seriously made, not quixotic or simply decided. President John Kennedy's decision to approve the trip to Dallas in November 1963 was a political calculation with enormous consequences for him and for the country. Texan political squabbles among Democrats could threaten his re-election and the trip to Texas was seen as an effort to mend those fences.

Similarly, President James Garfield's decision to travel from the train station where he was fatally shot in 1881 may fall into this category. Or President William McKinley deciding to attend the Panama American Exposition in Buffalo in 1901, where he was also fatally shot. It can be argued that Abraham Lincoln might have survived had he not attended the theater the night of his assassination in 1865, though John Wilkes Booth may have caught up with him elsewhere. But none of these scheduling decisions can be considered serious, strategic decisions.

Bill Clinton's decision to make private time for Monica Lewinsky had serious ramifications for both of them as well as for the country. When he lied about his sexual liaisons with her, he faced impeachment as a result. William Henry Harrison, America's ninth president, was dead only a month after his inauguration. His decision to ride in the inaugural parade coatless after finishing one of the longest inaugural orations ever, despite the wintery weather that day in Washington, likely led to the illness that felled him. None of these decisions can be considered deeply and strategically considered, though they were bad decisions.

It would have been appropriate to include the Bay of Pigs fiasco in 1961 to be the result of a bad decision by President Kennedy. People died, and it led to great hatred by many Cuban Americans toward JFK because he pulled the plug on the invasion and left the invaders stranded at the Bay of Pigs. But it also taught him a valuable lesson about the military. That lesson served him and us well in the way he resolved the Cuban Missile Crisis in 1962.

When President Gerald Ford, in 1974, decided to pardon his predecessor, Richard Nixon, it turned out to be a bad decision for Ford's political future but may be viewed as a good decision for the country. Ford understood the political risk but determined that the Watergate scandal needed to be put behind him and the country; the prosecution of Richard Nixon would consume his presidency. It is easy to see his decision as statesmanlike, looking at it from the vantage point of the 21st century.

Then. there was the process President Franklin Roosevelt went through to choose Harry Truman as his running mate in 1944. Roosevelt paid scant attention to the decision for Truman to join him on the ticket as he sought an unprecedented fourth term as president. He had been fed up with his Vice President Henry Wallace and left it up to other Democratic leaders to fill the second spot on the ticket. Wallace was someone FDR didn't like and knew that Democratic leaders considered him *too intellectual, too liberal, and too impractical*. However, FDR knew that his own health was in terrible shape, and it was unlikely he would survive the next four years. The president had been taken to Bethesda Naval Hospital, ostensibly to treat the symptoms of flu, and the examining doctor was horrified by what he found. As Roosevelt inhaled and exhaled with the doctor listening to a stethoscope, the physician heard *telltale rattling or bubbling sounds, indicating that fluid was building up inside the president's lungs…Roosevelt was literally starting the slow process of drowning from within* and the diagnosis was congestive heart failure. He was consumed with winning World War II, which is understandable, and was determined to run for re-election once again. [cclxvi]

After the Roosevelt-Truman ticket was elected, he didn't bring Truman into the counsels of war or share the secret of the atomic bomb with him. Both men, however, were aware of the president's physical condition. During the campaign, FDR had "instructed Truman to avoid airplanes because 'one of us needs to stay alive'." After the election, Truman was told by a friend that he would soon be president.

"I'm afraid you're right," he replied, "and it scares the hell out of me."[cclxvii]

Roosevelt had always been a realist and it's hard to understand how he could have let the choice of his successor be handled in such a cavalier manner. His selection for the vice presidency was made by party leaders with little involvement from the president. Truman had been a little-known U.S. senator from Missouri and served as vice president for less than three months when FDR died and he was thrust into the presidency.

It is easy to argue that Truman made wise decisions as president and served honorably, a decision that turned out well for the American people and for world history. One can argue that Truman became a great president, guiding the nation to an end of the war, and "would soon construct a foreign policy that ushered in the American Century while checking Joseph Stalin's designs on Western Europe." As former congressman and television anchor Joe Scarborough wrote shortly after the election of President Biden, "Truman's cumulative record is nothing short of astonishing. In a few short years, the 33rd president would champion the Truman Doctrine, the Marshall Plan, NATO and a visionary foreign policy that would define the United States' role on the world stage for 70 years."[cclxviii]

The president who was, perhaps, America's greatest, Abraham Lincoln, struggled with bad decisions during the Civil War, particularly in his choices among Union generals. He certainly made many great decisions that led to the eventual winning of that terrible war. He also made a number of good policy decisions during a presidency that was dominated by the war.

Among his good decisions were innovative programs like the Morrill Land Grant Act, establishing colleges, tariffs designed to encourage domestic manufacturing, land grants to provide funding for the first transcontinental railroad in the U.S., and the Homestead Act, to make land inexpensive for settlers migrating west.[cclxix]

The Homestead Act in 1862 allowed a settler free possession of 160 acres if farmed for five years. The legislation effectively transferred 80 million acres of public land into private hands and accommodated half a million people. American land policy resulted in the making of such states as Ohio, Indiana, and Illinois, the Middle West proper.[cclxx]

His choices for Union generals, on the other hand, were not decided well. Among them were Joseph Hooker, George B. McClellan, Irvin McDowell, Henry Halleck, and Ambrose Burnside. John Keegan wrote that, "Lincoln, a totally inexperienced commander in chief, was confronted at the outset of his presidency by a kaleidoscope of temperamental difficulties among his military helpmeets which would have brought down a lesser person. The verdict on the military leadership of the Union during the Civil War is that there was too much personality in play and far too little talent. Only Lincoln showed greatness from beginning to end. It was a war caused by his election and ultimately won by his capacity for compromise, an unexpected strategic skill."[cclxxi]

"Lincoln was besieged by men who wanted military appointments or, if they were already officers, promotion. They were supported by politicians from their states or their communities, particularly Germans, and their wives.

Of a wife who wanted her husband to be made a brigadier general, he wrote, 'She is a saucy woman, and I am afraid she will keep tormenting me until I may have to do it'. He did not object to being lobbied; from the beginning, he was anxious to identify men of talent, and he was prepared to try anyone in whom he glimpsed ability. The trouble was that such men were very rare and revealed themselves only in the harsh circumstances of battle. Far more numerous were men who accepted promotion, often offered for political reasons, but then expected the president to tell them what to do."[cclxxii]

"At the outset, however, he had the greatest difficulty in finding generals who displayed the least competence or resolution. He promoted dozens of men in 1861, though without confidence that any of them were good leaders, and often because their promotion would strengthen his political position." But what Lincoln wanted was a general, or generals, who had the "ability to achieve results without constantly requiring guidance from Washington or reinforcement by additional troops."[cclxxiii]

One of the more successful generals for the Union was William Tecumseh Sherman. He believed "that Lincoln should use the officers who had been serving on the western frontier. These men had practical experience that fitted them for commands. He was unimpressed with the president's recent choice of generals – Nathaniel Banks, John C. Fremont, John Pope, and others. 'Lincoln's present appointments do so plainly indicate a political bias that none but Union prone republicans should expect anything'. He wrote 'The appointment of Pope… etc. will afford to Bragg & David & Beauregard the liveliest pleasure. The north has so decided an advantage in men for the ranks that it is a pity to balance the chances by a choice of leaders…I know of no one competent unless it be [George B.] McClellan. But as soon as real war begins, new men, heretofore unheard of will emerge from obscurity, equal to any occasion'."[cclxxiv]

Lincoln's first three choices for generals to be in charge of the Army proved wrong. Irvin McDowell had been chosen to command at the first battle of Bull Run but was soon seen to lack the "force of character necessary to direct a large army in the field." George McClellan was chosen to replace McDowell, and he proved extremely popular with the soldiers and an excellent organizer and trainer of those soldiers. But he consistently called for reinforcements when he was heading into combat, despite the unquestioned fact that he had more men than the Confederate Army at that time. He seemed to lack "the killer instinct and could not," in a Lincolnian phrase, "put things through." There was one story about McClellan writing to Lincoln that his horses were tired. Lincoln responded that he couldn't imagine why they could possibly be tired. McClellan was building a great fighting force but could not get himself to force it to fight. Eventually, McClellan was replaced by Henry Halleck, known to his fellow West Point grads as *Old Brains*. He proved competent but hardly the leader that Lincoln knew he required in order to defeat the Confederacy. There were similar failures in the selections of commanders in secondary theaters of the war, men like John Fremont, Don Carlos Buell, Nathaniel Banks, and John Pope.[cclxxv]

After the disastrous defeat at Fredericksburg in December 1862, the general in charge, Ambrose Burnside, admitted full responsibility for it. The plans he made to repeat the assault that had already failed with great loss of life led two of his subordinates to go to Lincoln directly to express their fears about his plans. A conference was called at the White House on January 1, 1863, and Burnside unbelievably called for the resignations of General in-chief Henry Halleck and Secretary of War Stanton. At the same time, he admitted that his army had lost confidence in him and asked to be relieved. Burnside was sent back to his army without permission to repeat the assault and he began making wild accusations against some of his subordinates, including Joseph Hooker. Lincoln, before the month was out, replaced Burnside with Hooker.[cclxxvi]

Hooker led the Union Army in the battle of Chancellorsville. After the battle, as Confederate General Robert E. Lee led his men into Pennsylvania, Lincoln was sorely disappointed that Hooker had not taken the steps to oppose the advance. Hooker made things worse by proposing to Lincoln that he abandon the Virginia theater completely and turn his attention to taking the Confederate capital at Richmond. By this time, in June 1893, Lincoln had begun taking the reins of military leadership to himself. When Lincoln received Hooker's proposal on June 10, he fired off a reply within 90 minutes. It was, in the words of John Keegan, "one of the very best pieces of strategic judgement written during the war. 'I think Lee's army, and not Richmond, is your true objective point. If he comes toward the upper Potomac, follow on his flank, and on the inside track, shortening your lines whilst he lengthens his…If he stays where he is, fret him, and fret him'."[cclxxvii]

It wasn't until he chose Ulysses S. Grant, after his stirring victories at Shiloh and Vicksburg, that he had the fighting general he so desperately wanted and needed. Grant would end up as the victorious military leader in the Civil War.

Among the greatest of bad decisions in American history was Abraham Lincoln's choice of Tennessee Governor Andrew Johnson as his running mate in the 1864 re-election campaign. Johnson was seen as a unifying choice during the Civil War, a pro-Union southern governor. After the successful re-election, at Lincoln's second inaugural, Johnson appeared to be inebriated. This horrified many people in attendance but the better description as to why Johnson's selection was a bad decision goes to the period after Lincoln's assassination in 1865.

Johnson's racist attitudes soon became known after he acceded to the presidency; he did not follow the plan of Reconstruction that was believed to be Lincoln's, and the legacy of that period has resonated negatively throughout American society ever since. Lincoln had hoped to heal the nation's wounds. Johnson exacerbated them.

President Andrew Johnson made decisions leading to his impeachment. A very stubborn man, he probably never felt those decisions were bad ones. He considered the law requiring Congressional approval in order to remove cabinet officials who had been previously confirmed by the Senate to be unconstitutional. The Supreme Court later proved him right, but his defiance of the law and removal of Secretary of War Edwin Stanton led to the first presidential impeachment in our nation's history. He was unceremoniously dropped from the Republican ticket for president in 1868.

There are clearly other bad decisions in American history that can be chronicled. Many bad decisions have been made in political campaigns that led to the bad decider's defeat. Some have been included here but there are clearly others. Often, a candidate appears to mis-speak but the miscalculation leading to the particular statement often was the result of serious thought that turned out to be in error. Others may have been strategic, like when former New York mayor Rudy Giuliani decided to wait until the Florida primary to enter the 2008 Republican nominating contest. By that date, the nomination had been secured by Sen. John McCain. That chapter could have been called, 'He Who Hesitates is Lost'.

Campaign decisions gone awry have occurred in many modern campaigns and could have been included here.

1948: Republican nominee Thomas Dewey decided to *play it safe* against President Harry Truman. He believed the polls taken at the time, now known to be seriously flawed, and instead of taking on the president, he thought he would coast to the election. He lost and Truman pulled off one of the greatest upsets in presidential campaign history.

1964: New York Governor Nelson Rockefeller, a presidential aspirant in 1964 and 1968, decided against running negative ads against Arizona Senator Barry Goldwater, helping Goldwater find the successful path to the Republican presidential nomination.

1968: Michigan Governor George Romney, hoping to unseat President Lyndon Johnson from the White House, created a crisis that killed his candidacy when describing his experience with the Vietnam War as having *brainwashed* him.

1972: South Dakota Senator George McGovern won the Democratic presidential nomination and chose as his running mate Missouri Senator Thomas Eagleton. Not having vetted him well, news of Eagleton's bout with mental illness led him to resign from the ticket. Just prior to that resignation, McGovern announced he was "*1,000 percent*" behind Eagleton, a statement that haunted him for the remainder of a disastrous campaign.

1976: President Gerald Ford damaged his own election prospects by pardoning former President Richard Nixon. While the act may be considered statesmanlike, it clearly damaged his political prospects. He had to fight for the Republican nomination that year against former California Governor Ronald Reagan, who made his own bad decision that damaged his nomination effort by choosing Pennsylvania Senator Richard Schweiker as his running mate. Reagan's conservative supporters were appalled by their hero's choice of a liberal senator to be vice president and Ford won the nomination. But Ford tried to appeal to the more conservative faction of his party by dropping his own vice president from the ticket. Vice President Nelson Rockefeller was replaced by Senator Bob Dole, something Ford later described as "the worst decision of his presidency."[cclxxviii] Another bad decision that year was by the Democratic nominee, former Georgia Governor Jimmy Carter. Carter, an evangelical Christian who was dominating the polls at the time, gave an ill-advised interview with *Playboy* magazine, nearly submarining his own election.

1980: President Jimmy Carter damaged his own re-election prospects by statements made during his debates with the Republican nominee, Ronald Reagan. One egregious example was when he said that he consulted with his young daughter Amy about the most serious issues facing the country. Then, after losing the election, on election night he conceded before the polls closed on the West Coast, helping to defeat some Democratic Congressional candidates when their voters heard the election was over and they left their places in lines at the polling locations.

1988: Democratic presidential nominee, Massachusetts Governor Michael Dukakis contributed a series of miss-steps that led to his election defeat against Vice President George H. W. Bush after having a strong lead in national polling. There was a campaign ad where Dukakis allowed himself to look ridiculous in a helmet driving a tank. There was the decision not to use an ad highlighting the Bush wealth or focusing on Bush's choice for a running mate,

Indiana Senator Dan Quayle, highly controversial at the time. Also, Dukakis decided he couldn't stop working as a governor and spent 4 days per week doing so – throughout the campaign.

2012: The 47% statement made by former Massachusetts Governor Mitt Romney, referred to in the preface, clearly had a negative impact on his election prospects against the Democratic nominee, President Barack Obama.

2016: When former First Lady and Secretary of State Hillary Clinton, the Democratic presidential nominee running against Republican Donald Trump, characterized his supporters as *"deplorables,"* it fueled the opposition against her, leading to a narrow defeat in the Electoral College though winning the popular vote.

2022: Two years into the Joseph Biden presidency, when many Americans assumed he would only serve a single term, his decision to run for re-election in 2024 was a bad one. When he shifted gears after a disastrous debate performance, the 81-year-old president withdrew from the campaign. It led to a hasty process to have Vice President Kamala Harris replace him on the ticket, which proved unsuccessful in an election against former President Donald Trump.

Perhaps, what constitutes a bad decision is in the eye of the beholder. Historians can argue these points forever. But to err is human and the unforced errors listed here will not be the last ones.

Unforced Errors:
15 Bad Decisions That Changed American History A Bibliography

Alter, Jonathan, <u>His Very Best: Jimmy Carter, A Life</u>, Simon & Schuster, New York, 2020

Anson, Robert Sam, <u>Exile: The Unquiet Oblivion of Richard M. Nixon</u>, Simon & Schuster, New York, 1984

Bemis, Samuel Flagg, <u>John Quincy Adams and The Union</u>, Volume II, Alfred A. Knopf, Inc., New York, 1956

Berg, A. Scott, <u>Wilson,</u> G.P. Putnam's Sons, New York, 2013

Brands, H.W., <u>Founding Partisans: Hamilton, Madison, Jefferson, Adams and the Brawling Birth of American Politics</u>, Doubleday, New York, 2023

Brodie, Fawn M., <u>Richard Nixon: The Shaping of His Character</u>, W.W. Norton & Co., New York, 1981

Brown, Daniel James, <u>Facing the Mountain</u>, Viking, New York, 2021

Burns, James MacGregor, <u>Roosevelt: The Lion and the Fox: Volume I</u>, Harcourt, Brace, Jovanovich, Inc., New York, 1956

Bush, George W., <u>Decision Points</u>, Crown Publishers, New York, 2010

Clinton, William J., <u>My Life</u>, Alfred A. Knopf, New York, 2004

Cooper, John Milton Jr., <u>Woodrow Wilson: A Biography</u>, Alfred A. Knopf, New York, 2009

Dallek, Robert, <u>An Unfinished Life: John F. Kennedy 1917-1963,</u> Little, Brown and Company, New York, 2003

Dallek, Robert, <u>Flawed Giant: Lyndon Johnson and His Times 1961-1973</u>, Oxford University Press, New York, 1998

Dunn, Arthur Wallace, <u>From Harrison to Harding,</u> Vol. 1, G. P. Putnam & Sons, New York, 1922

Eig, Jonathan, <u>King: A Life</u>, Farrar, Straus and Giroux, New York, 2023

Ellis, Joseph, <u>First Family</u>, Alfred A. Knopf, New York, 2010

Ellis, Joseph, <u>Passionate Sage</u>, W.W. Norton & Company, New York, 1993

Ferling, John, <u>Adams vs. Jefferson: The Tumultuous Election of 1800</u>, Oxford University Press, New York, 2004

Gage, Beverly, <u>G-Man: J. Edgar Hoover and the Making of the American Century</u>, Viking, New York, 2022

Goodwin, Doris Kearns, <u>An Unfinished Love Story: A Personal History of the 1960s</u>, Simon & Schuster, New York, 2024

Goodwin, Doris Kearns, <u>No Ordinary Time</u>, Simon & Schuster, New York, 1994

Goodwin, Doris Kearns, <u>The Bully Pulpit</u>, Simon & Schuster, New York, 2013

Holzer, Harold and Garfinkle, Norton, <u>A Just And Generous Nation</u>, Basic Books, New York, 2015

Horner, William T., Ohio's Kingmaker: Mark Hanna, Man and Myth, Ohio University Press, Athens, OH, 2010

James, Marquis, Andrew Jackson: Portrait of a President, The Easton Press by arrangement with The Bobbs-Merrill Company, Norwalk, CT, 1937

James, Marquis, Andrew Jackson: The Border Captain, The Easton Press by arrangement with The Bobbs-Merrill Company, Norwalk, CT, 1933

Kearns, Doris, Lyndon Johnson & The American Dream, Harper & Row, New York, 1976

Keegan, John, The American Civil War, Knopf, New York, 2009

Keegan, John, The Iraq War, Vintage Books, London, 2005

Kerry, John, Every Day is Extra, Simon & Schuster, New York, 2018

Krock, Arthur, Memoirs, Funk & Wagnalls, New York, 1968

Leebaert, Derek, Unlikely Heroes, St. Martins Press, New York, 2023

Lincoln, Evelyn, My Twelve Years with John F. Kennedy, David McKay Company, Inc., New York, 1965

McAuliffe, Terry, What a Party!, Thomas Dunne Books, New York, 2007

McCullough, David, John Adams, Simon & Schuster, New York, 2001

Meachum, Jon, American Lion: Andrew Jackson in the White House, Random House, New York, 2008

Merrill, James M., William Tecumseh Sherman, Rand McNally & Company, New York, 1971

Morris, Edmund, Colonel Roosevelt, Random House, New York, 2010

Morris, Edmund, The Rise of Theodore Roosevelt, Ballantine Books, New York, 1979

Morris, Edmund, Theodore Rex, Random House, New York, 2001

Nixon, Richard M., RN: The Memoirs of Richard Nixon, Warner Books, Inc., New York, 1978

O'Donnell, Kenneth P. and Powers, David F. with McCarthy, Joe, Johnny, We Hardly Knew Ye, Little, Brown & Company, Boston, 1970

Parmet, Herbert S., George Bush: The Life of a Lone Star Yankee, Simon & Schuster, New York, 1997

Parmet, Herbert S., Jack: The Struggles of John F. Kennedy, The Easton Press with permission of Doubleday and Company, Norwalk, CT, 1980

Peterson, Merrill D., Lincoln in American Memory, Oxford University Press, New York, 1994

Pringle, Henry F., The Life and Times of William Howard Taft, The Easton Press by arrangement with Holt, Rinehart and Winston, Norwalk, CT, 1939

Pringle, Henry F., Theodore Roosevelt, Harcourt Brace Jovanovich, Inc., New York, 1931

Reedy, George E., The Twilight of the Presidency, The New American Library, New York, 1970

Reeves, Richard, President Kennedy: Profile of Power, Simon & Schuster, New York, 1993

Remini, Robert V., The Life of Andrew Jackson, Harper & Row, New York, 1988

Remnick, David, <u>The Bridge: The Life and Rise of Barack Obama</u>, Alfred A. Knopf, New York, 2010

Ricks, Thomas E., <u>First Principles,</u> Harper Collins, New York, 2020

Risen, James, <u>The Last Honest Man,</u> Little, Brown & Company, New York, 2023

Shenkman, Richard & Reiger, Kurt, <u>One-Night Stands with American History,</u> William Morrow & Co., New York, 1980

Sidey, Hugh, <u>John F. Kennedy, President</u>, Atheneum, New York, 1963

Smith, Jean Edward, <u>FDR</u>, Random House, New York, 2007

Smith, Page, <u>John Adams; Volume I</u>, The Easton Press, Norwalk, CT, 1962

Sorensen, Theodore C., <u>Kennedy</u>, Harper & Row Publishers, New York, 1965

Steinem, Gloria, <u>My Life on the Road</u>, Random House, New York, 2015

Takiff, Michael, <u>A Complicated Man: The Life of Bill Clinton as Told by Those Who Know Him,</u> Yale University Press, New Haven, 2010

Taliaferro, John, <u>All the Great Prizes: The Life of John Hay, from Lincoln to Roosevelt</u>, Simon & Schuster, New York, 2013

Traub, James, <u>John Quincy Adams: Militant Spirit</u>, Basic Books, New York, 2016

Walworth, Arthur, <u>Woodrow Wilson: American Prophet</u>, W.W. Norton & Co., New York, 1958

Warren, Earl, <u>The Memoirs of Earl Warren</u>, Doubleday, New York, 1977

White, Theodore H., <u>Breach of Faith: The Fall of Richard Nixon</u>, Atheneum Publishers, New York, 1975

White, Theodore H., <u>The Making of the President 1960</u>, Atheneum Publishers, New York, 1961

Young, James Sterling, <u>The Washington Community: 1800-1828</u>, Columbia University Press, New York and London, 1966

References

[i] McCullough, David, *John Adams*, Simon & Schuster, New York, 2001, page 468

[ii] McCullough, *John Adams*, page 504

[iii] Ferling, John *Adams vs. Jefferson: The Tumultuous Election of 1800,* Oxford University Press, 2004, page 122

[iv] McCullough, *John Adams*, page 505

[v] Ricks, Thomas E., *First Principles*, Harper Collins, 2020, page 240

[vi] Ricks, *First Principles,* page 241

[vii] Shenkman, Richard & Reiger, Kurt, *One-Night Stands with American History,* William Morrow & Co., New York, 1980, pages 47–48

[viii] Brands, H.W., *Founding Partisans: Hamilton, Madison, Jefferson, Adams and the Brawling Birth of American Politics,* Doubleday, New York, 2023, page 345

[ix] McCullough, *John Adams*, page 506

[x] McCullough , *John Adams*, page 521

[xi] Ferling, *Adams vs. Jefferson: The Tumultuous Election of 1800,* page 112

[xii] Ferling, *Adams vs. Jefferson: The Tumultuous Election of 1800*, page 111

[xiii] McCullough, *John Adams*, page 285

[xiv] Ferling, *Adams vs. Jefferson: The Tumultuous Election of 1800,* page 111

[xv] Brockell, Gillian, "A history of presidential rages and tantrums, from Adams to Trump," *The Washington Post*, July 5, 2022, page B4.

[xvi] Ellis, Joseph, *Passionate Sage*, W.W. Norton & Company, New York, 1993, page 235

[xvii] Bemis, Samuel Flagg, *John Quincy Adams and The Union*, Volume II, Alfred A. Knopf, Inc., New York, 1956, page 11

[xviii] Traub, James, *John Quincy Adams: Militant Spirit*, Basic Books, New York, 2016, page 300

[xix] Bemis, *John Quincy Adams and The Union*, Volume II, page 16

[xx] Bemis, *John Quincy Adams and The Union*, Volume II, page 18

[xxi] Bemis, *John Quincy Adams and The Union*, Volume II, page 19

[xxii] *Race for the White House*, CNN, March-April 2016

xxiii Traub, *John Quincy Adams: Militant Spirit*, page 306

xxiv Bemis, *John Quincy Adams and The Union*, Volume II, page 38

xxv Bemis, *John Quincy Adams and The Union*, Volume II, page 57

xxvi Meachem, Jon, American Lion: Andrew Jackson in the White House, Random House, New York, 2008, page 80

xxvii Young, James Sterling, *The Washington Community: 1800–1828*, Columbia University Press, New York and London, 1966, page 243

xxviii McCullough, *John Adams*, page 447

xxix Taliaferro, *All the Great Prizes: The Life of John Hay, from Lincoln to Roosevelt*, page 259

xxx Taliaferro, *All the Great Prizes: The Life of John Hay, from Lincoln to Roosevelt*, pages 201–204

xxxi Morris, Edmund, *The Rise of Theodore Roosevelt*, Ballantine Books, New York, 1979, pages 516–518.

xxxii *Theodore Roosevelt: The Great Adventure*, The History Channel, Episode 1, May 30, 2022

xxxiii Bobelian, Michael, "A friendship that defined an era – and was tested by politics," *The Washington Post*, July 2, 2023, page B5

xxxiv Morris, *The Rise of Theodore Roosevelt*, pages 516–712

xxxv Morris, *The Rise of Theodore Roosevelt*, page 719

xxxvi Taliaferro, *All the Great Prizes: The Life of John Hay, from Lincoln to Roosevelt*, pages 375–376

xxxvii Dunn, Arthur Wallace, *From Harrison to Harding, Vol. 1*, G. P. Putnam & Sons, New York, 1922, pages 334–335

xxxviii Horner, William T., *Ohio's Kingmaker: Mark Hanna, Man and Myth*, Ohio University Press, Athens, OH, 2010, page 266

xxxix Taliaferro, *All the Great Prizes: The Life of John Hay, from Lincoln to Roosevelt*, page 389

xl Bobelian, "A friendship that defined an era – and was tested by politics," page B5

xli Morris, Edmund, *Theodore Rex*, Random House, New York, 2001, page 362

xlii Goodwin, Doris Kearns, *The Bully Pulpit*, Simon & Schuster, New York, 2013, page 2

xliii Morris, *Theodore Rex*, page 364

xliv PBS, The American Experience, *TR*, produced by David Grubin, 1996

xlv The History Channel, "Theodore Roosevelt – The Man in the Arena," Episode 2, May 31, 2022

xlvi Morris, *Theodore Rex*, page 521

xlvii Morris, *Theodore Rex*, page 554

xlviii Goodwin, *The Bully Pulpit*, page xi

xlix Morris, *Theodore Rex*, page 554

[l] Pringle, Henry F., *Theodore Roosevelt*, Harcourt Brace Jovanovich, Inc., New York, 1931, page 477

[li] Goodwin, *The Bully Pulpit*, pages 2–3

[lii] Goodwin, *The Bully Pulpit*, page 13

[liii] Pringle, *Theodore Roosevelt*, pages 534–535

[liv] Goodwin, *The Bully Pulpit*, page 17

[lv] Goodwin, *The Bully Pulpit*, pages 672–675

[lvi] Goodwin, *The Bully Pulpit*, page 677

[lvii] Goodwin, *The Bully Pulpit*, pages 696-697

[lviii] Goodwin, *The Bully Pulpit*, pages 703, 712

[lix] Bobelian, "A friendship that defined an era – and was tested by politics," page B5

[lx] Goodwin, *The Bully Pulpit*, page 737

[lxi] Goodwin, *The Bully Pulpit*, page 740

[lxii] Goodwin, *The Bully Pulpit*, page 745

[lxiii] Bobelian, "A friendship that defined an era – and was tested by politics," page B5

[lxiv] Goodwin, *The Bully Pulpit*, pages 746 & 748

[lxv] Berg, A. Scott, *Wilson*, G.P. Putnam's Sons, New York, 2013, page 505

[lxvi] Berg, *Wilson*, page 469

[lxvii] Berg, *Wilson*, page 470

[lxviii] Berg, *Wilson*, page 471

[lxix] Berg, *Wilson*, page 504

[lxx] Walworth, Arthur, *Woodrow Wilson: American Prophet*, W.W. Norton & Co., New York, 1958, page 344

[lxxi] Walworth, *Woodrow Wilson: American Prophet*, page 425

[lxxii] Krock, Arthur, *Memoirs*, Funk & Wagnalls, New York, 1968, page 38

[lxxiii] Berg, *Wilson,* page 566

[lxxiv] Berg, *Wilson,* page 578

[lxxv] Cooper, John Milton Jr., *Woodrow Wilson: A Biography*, Alfred A. Knopf, New York, 2009, page 11

[lxxvi] Berg, *Wilson,* page 585

[lxxvii] Cooper, *Woodrow Wilson: A Biography,* page 7

[lxxviii] Cooper, *Woodrow Wilson: A Biography*, page 4

[lxxix] Walworth, *Woodrow Wilson: American Prophet*, page 425

[lxxx] Berg, *Wilson,* page 517

[lxxxi] Berg, *Wilson,* page 518

[lxxxii] Berg, *Wilson,* page 592

[lxxxiii] Ginsberg, Gary, "'First buddy': A cautionary precedent," *The Washington Post*, January 23, 2025, page A17

[lxxxiv] Berg, *Wilson,* page 601

[lxxxv] Berg, *Wilson*, pages 609–611

[lxxxvi] Berg, *Wilson,* page 619

[lxxxvii] Berg, *Wilson,* page 649

[lxxxviii] Berg, *Wilson,* page 679

[lxxxix] Reedy, George E., *The Twilight of the Presidency,* The New American Library, New York, 1970, page 142

[xc] Weil, Julie Zauzmer, "Black family unravels mystery of 1879 wedding," *The Washington Post*, 25 October 2022, page A10

[xci] Brown, Daniel James, *Facing the Mountain*, Viking, 2021, page 43

[xcii] Gage, Beverly, *G-Man: J. Edgar Hoover and the Making of the American Century*, Viking, New York, 2022, page 258

[xciii] Brown, *Facing the Mountain*, page 44

[xciv] https://www.archives.gov/milestone-documents/executive-order-9066

[xcv] Brown, *Facing the Mountain*, page 25

[xcvi] Brown, *Facing the Mountain*, pages 86–87

[xcvii] Brown, *Facing the Mountain*, page 59

[xcviii] Risen, James, *The Last Honest Man,* Little, Brown & Company, New York, 2023, page 30

[xcix] Brown, *Facing the Mountain*, page 124

[c] Brown, *Facing the Mountain*, page 140

[ci] Brown*, Facing the Mountain*, page 132

[cii] https://www.archives.gov/milestone-documents/executive-order-9066

[ciii] Leebaert, Derek, *Unlikely Heroes*, St. Martins Press, New York, 2023, pages 337–338

[civ] Leebaert, *Unlikely Heroes*, page 388

[cv] Leebaert, *Unlikely Heroes*, page 401

[cvi] Brown, *Facing the Mountain*, page 378

[cvii] Brown, *Facing the Mountain*, page 466

[cviii] Brown, *Facing the Mountain*, page 468

[cix] Brown, *Facing the Mountain*, pages 469–474

[cx] Brown, *Facing the Mountain*, page 466

[cxi] Smith, Jean Edward, *FDR*, Random House, New York, 2007, page 528

[cxii] Smith, *FDR*, page 549

[cxiii] Smith, *FDR*, page 550

[cxiv] Warren, Earl, *The Memoirs of Earl Warren*, Doubleday, New York, 1977, page 149

[cxv] Smith, *FDR*, page 551

[cxvi] Smith, *FDR*, pages 773–774

[cxvii] Gage, *G-Man: J. Edgar Hoover and the Making of the American Century*, page 57

[cxviii] Gage, *G-Man: J. Edgar Hoover and the Making of the American Century*, pages 258–260

cxix Goodwin, Doris Kearns, *No Ordinary Time*, Simon & Schuster, New York, 1994, pages 321–323

cxx Smith, *FDR*, pages 552–553

cxxi Burns, James MacGregor, *Roosevelt: The Lion and the Fox*, Harcourt, Brace, Jovanovich, Inc., New York, 1956, page 463

cxxii Dallek, Robert, *An Unfinished Life: John F. Kennedy 1917–1963,* Little, Brown and Company, New York, 2003, pages 279–280

cxxiii Sorensen, Theodore C., *Kennedy,* Harper & Row Publishers, New York, 1965, page 198

cxxiv White, Theodore H., *The Making of the President 1960*, Atheneum Publishers, New York, 1961, pages 309–310

cxxv *Race for the White House: 1960 John F. Kennedy vs Richard Nixon*, CNN, March-April, 2016, Season 1, Episode 1

cxxvi Lepore, Jill, *The State of Debate*, *The New Yorker*, September 19, 2016, page 38

cxxvii Goodwin, Doris Kearns, *An Unfinished Love Story: A Personal History of the 1960s,* Simon & Schuster, New York, 2024, page 64

cxxviii White, *The Making of the President 1960*, page 306

cxxix *Race for the White House: 1960 John F. Kennedy vs Richard Nixon*, Season 1, Episode 1

cxxx White, *The Making of the President 1960*, pages 318–319

cxxxi White, *The Making of the President 1960*, pages 321–322

cxxxii O'Donnell, Kenneth P. and Powers, David F. with McCarthy, Joe, *Johnny,_We Hardly Knew Ye*, Little, Brown & Company, Boston, 1970, page 211

cxxxiii Krock, Arthur, *Memoirs*, Funk & Wagnalls, New York, 1968, page 369

cxxxiv Peterson, Merrill D., *Lincoln in American Memory*, Oxford University Press, New York, 1994, page 326

cxxxv Goodwin, *An Unfinished Love Story: A Personal History of the 1960s*, pages 66–67

cxxxvi Lepore, *The State of Debate*, page 40

cxxxvii Nixon, Richard M., *RN: The Memoirs of Richard Nixon*, Warner Books, Inc., New York, 1978, pages 217–219

cxxxviii Sorensen, *Kennedy*, pages 196–198

cxxxix Lepore, *The State of Debate*, page 42

cxl Anson, Robert Sam, *Exile: The Unquiet Oblivion of Richard M. Nixon*, Simon & Schuster, New York, 1984, page 227

cxli Kearns, Doris, *Lyndon Johnson & The American Dream*, Harper & Row, New York, 1976, page 263

cxlii Goodman, Walter, *Commentary* magazine, April 1969

cxliii Kearns, *Lyndon Johnson & The American Dream*, page 226 cxliv Dallek, Robert, *Flawed Giant: Lyndon Johnson and His Times 1961–1973*, Oxford University Press, New York, 1998, page 340

cxlv Dallek, *Flawed Giant: Lyndon Johnson and His Times 1961–1973*, page 340

cxlvi Kearns, *Lyndon Johnson & The American Dream,* page 100

cxlvii Kearns, *Lyndon Johnson & The American Dream*, pages 264–265

cxlviii Eig, Jonathan, *King: A Life*, Farrar, Straus and Giroux, New York, 2023, pages 428–429

cxlix Reedy, *The Twilight of the Presidency*, page 133

cl Kearns, *Lyndon Johnson & The American Dream*, pages 240–241

cli Eig, *King: A Life,* page 448

clii Eig*, King: A Life*, page 508

cliii Eig, *King: A Life*, page 542

cliv Kearns, *Lyndon Johnson & The American Dream*, page 263

clv Kearns*, Lyndon Johnson & The American Dream*, page xiii

clvi Goodwin, *An Unfinished Love Story: A Personal History of the 1960s*, pages 330–331

clvii Kearns, *Lyndon Johnson & The American Dream*, page 326

clviii Eig, *King: A Life*, page 529

clix Kearns, *Lyndon Johnson & The American Dream*, pages 416–417

clx Kearns, *Lyndon Johnson & The American Dream*, page 425

clxi Kearns, *Lyndon Johnson & The American Dream*, page 299

clxii Nixon, Richard M., *RN: The Memoirs of Richard Nixon*, The Easton Press, Norwalk, CT, 1978, pages 670–671

clxiii Nixon, *RN: The Memoirs of Richard Nixon*, page 646

clxiv Brodie, Fawn M., *Richard Nixon: The Shaping of His Character*, W.W. Norton & Co., New York, 1981, page 23

clxv Brodie, *Richard Nixon: The Shaping of His Character*, page 504

clxvi Brockell, Gillian, "Kissinger held a sobbing Nixon before the president resigned, book says," *The Washington Post*, December 1, 2023, page B6

clxvii Nixon, *RN: The Memoirs of Richard Nixon*, page 680

clxviii Nixon, *RN: The Memoirs of Richard Nixon,* page 870

clxvix Nixon, RN: The Memoirs of Richard Nixon, page 824

clxx White, Theodore H., *Breach of Faith: The Fall of Richard Nixon*, Atheneum Publishers, New York, 1975, pages 209–210.

clxxi Nixon, *RN: The Memoirs of Richard Nixon*, pages 849–851

clxxii Nixon, *RN: The Memoirs of Richard Nixon*, page 871

clxxiii Anson, Robert Sam, *Exile: The Unquiet Oblivion of Richard M. Nixon,* Simon & Schuster, New York, 1984, page 86

clxxiv Nixon, *RN: The Memoirs of Richard Nixon,* pages 901–903

clxxv Nixon, *RN: The Memoirs of Richard Nixon,* pages 990–991 [clxxvi] Nixon, *RN: The Memoirs of Richard Nixon*, page 995

[clxxvii] Nixon, *RN: The Memoirs of Richard Nixon*, page 1004

[clxxviii] Nixon, *RN: The Memoirs of Richard Nixon*, page 1027

[clxxix] Nixon, *RN: The Memoirs of Richard Nixon*, page 1051

[clxxx] Anson, *Exile: The Unquiet Oblivion of Richard M. Nixon*, page 269

[clxxxi] Brodie, *Richard Nixon: The Shaping of His Character,* page 511

[clxxxii] Anson, *Exile: The Unquiet Oblivion of Richard M. Nixon,* page 264

[clxxxiii] Anson, *Exile: The Unquiet Oblivion of Richard M. Nixon,* page 270

[clxxxiv] Curtis, Bruce, "The Wimp Factor,*"* *American Heritage*, November 1989, Volume 40, Issue 7

[clxxxv] Elving, Ron, "6 Little Words Helped Make George H.W. Bush (A 1-Term) President," National Public Radio All Things Considered, December 4, 2018

[clxxxvi] Parmet, Herbet S., *George Bush: The Life of a Lone Star Yankee,* Simon & Schuster, New York, 1997, page 365

[clxxxvii] Kranish, Michael, "In N.H., GOP hopefuls once took a starkly different stance on environment," *The Washington Post*, January 22, 2024, page A8

[clxxxviii] Parmet, *George Bush: The Life of a Lone Star Yankee,* page 322

[clxxxix] Parmet, *George Bush: The Life of a Lone Star Yankee*, page 337

[cxc] Parmet, *George Bush: The Life of a Lone Star Yankee,* page 338

[cxci] Parmet, *George Bush: The Life of a Lone Star Yankee*, page 367

[cxcii] Kramer, Michael, "A New Breeze is Blowing," *Time* Magazine, January 30, 1989, page 20

[cxciii] Parmet, *George Bush: The Life of a Lone Star Yankee*, page 348

[cxciv] Parmet, *George Bush: The Life of a Lone Star Yankee*, page 361

[cxcv] Kramer, "A New Breeze is Blowing," page 19

[cxcvi] Parmet, *George Bush: The Life of a Lone Star Yankee*, page 435

[cxcvii] Parmet, *George Bush: The Life of a Lone Star Yankee,* pages 468–469

[cxcviii] Parmet, *George Bush: The Life of a Lone Star Yankee,* page 470

[cxcix] Clinton, William J., *My Life,* Alfred A. Knopf, New York, 2004, Pagepage 420

[cc] Clinton, *My Life*, page 427

[cci] Clinton, *My Life,* page 430

[ccii] Elving, "6 Little Words Helped Make George H.W. Bush (A 1-Term) President,"

[cciii] "Top 10 Unfortunate Political One-Liners," *Time* Magazine, November 17, 2008

[cciv] Rothman, Lilly, "The Story Behind George H.W. Bush's Famous 'Read my Lips, No New Taxes Promise," *Time* Magazine, December 1, 2018

[ccv] Clinton, My Life, pages 910-911

[ccvi] Clinton, *My Life*, pages 911

[ccvii] McAuliffe, Terry, *What a Party!,* Thomas Dunne Books, New York, 2007, page 236

ccviii Smith, Sally Bedell, "White House Civil War," *Vanity Fair*, October 1, 2007, page 15

ccix Smith, "White House Civil War," page 4

ccx Nichols, Bill, "Clinton and Gore: Still the odd couple," *Politico*, September 27, 2009, page 6

ccxi Smith, "White House Civil War," page 3

ccxii Smith, "White House Civil War," page 4

ccxiii Smith, "White House Civil War," page 5

ccxiv Smith, "White House Civil War," pages 8–9

ccxv Smith, "White House Civil War," page 11

ccxvi Smith, "White House Civil War," page 11

ccxvii Smith, "White House Civil War," page 14

ccxviii Clinton, *My Life*, pages 918

ccxix Smith, "White House Civil War," page 16

ccxx Harris, John F., "Clinton and Gore Clashed Over Blame for Election," *The Washington Post*, February 7, 2001

ccxxi Harris, "Clinton and Gore Clashed Over Blame for Election"

ccxxii Smith, "White House Civil War," page 18

ccxxiii Smith, "White House Civil War," page 20

ccxxiv Smith, "White House Civil War," page 20

ccxxv Harris, "Clinton and Gore Clashed Over Blame for Election"

ccxxvi Nichols, "Clinton and Gore: Still the odd couple," page 2

ccxxvii Balz, Dan, "Gore Calls 2000 Verdict 'Crushing', Assails Court," *The Washington Post*, November 15, 2002

ccxxviii Takiff, Michael, *A Complicated Man: The Life of Bill Clinton as Told by Those Who Know Him,* Yale University Press, New Haven, 2010, pages 392–395

ccxxvix Von Drehle, David and Smith, R. Jeffrey, "U.S. Strikes Iraq for Plot to Kill Bush," The Washington Post, June 27, 1993, page A1

ccxxx Bush, George W., *Decision Points*, Crown Publishers, New York, 2010, pages 188–190

ccxxxi Bush, *Decision Points*, page 158

ccxxxii Keegan, John, *The Iraq War*, Vintage Books, London, 2005, page 169

ccxxxiii Bush, *Decision Points*, , pages 228–9

ccxxxiv Bush, *Decision Points*, page 236

ccxxxv Bush, *Decision Points*, page 232

ccxxxvi Statements of the Director General, IAEA, March 6, 2003

ccxxxvii *UN News*, September 16, 2004

ccxxxviii *Chilcot report: Findings at-a-glance*, BBC News, July 6, 2011

ccxxxix "Little evidence for Iraq WMDs ahead of 2003 war: U.S. declassified report," *International Business Times*, February 8, 2011

ccxl CNN Inside Politics, October 2, 2002

ccxli "Attacks in Iraq at All-Time High, Pentagon Says," *Newshour*, PBS, December 19, 2006

ccxlii Trotta, Daniel, "Iraq war hits U.S. economy: Nobel winner," *Reuters,* March 2, 2008

ccxliii Sengupta, Kim, "Occupation Made World Less Safe, Pro-War Institute Says," *The Independent,* May 26, 2004

ccxliv Ackerman, Spencer, "The pragmatic side of Saddam Hussein," *The Washington Post*, March 3, 2004, pages B1 and B7

ccxlv Robinson, Linda, "The Long Shadow of the Iraq War: Lessons and Legacies Twenty Years Later," Council of Foreign Relations, March 20, 2023

ccxlvi Fazil, Shivan and Tartir, Dr. Alaa, "Iraq in 2023: Challenges and prospects for peace and human security," SIPRI, March 17, 2023

ccxlvii Kerry, John F., Vietnam Veterans Against the War Speech Before the U.S. Senate Committee on Foreign Relations, April 22, 1971, reprinted by Voices of Democracy, The U.S. Oratory Project

ccxlviii RoperCenter.Cornell.edu/2004presidentialelection

ccxlix Bush, *Decision Points*, page 288

ccl Encylopedia.Com, "Swift Boat Veterans for Truth Campaign Overview"

ccli McAuliffe, *What a Party!*, page 355

cclii Kerry, John, *Every Day is Extra*, Simon & Schuster, New York, 2018, pages 301–306

ccliii Remnick, David, *The Bridge: The Life and Rise of Barack Obama*, Alfred A. Knopf, New York, 2010, page 417

ccliv NBCNews.Com, "Kerry vows to disprove Swift Boat claims," November 16, 2007

cclv Gambino, Lauren, "John McCain: 10 moments that will shape the senator's legacy," *The Guardian*, August 25, 2018, www.TheGuardian.Com/US-News/2018/Aug/25/John-McCain-Death-Moments-Life-Shape-Legacy

cclvi "The Contenders: 16 for '16," PBS, September-October 2016

cclvii Cleary, Patrick, "Sarah Palin and her overarching impact on our political landscape," *The Spectator*, April 14, 2022

cclviii Brown, Michael H., "A four-term U.S. senator who went his own way," *The Washington Post*, March 28, 2024, page A15

cclix Milbank, Dana, "The Mother of the Trump Movement? You Betcha – It Was Her," *The Washington Post,* May 12, 2016

cclx Remnick, *The Bridge: The Life and Rise of Barack Obama*, pages 554–555

cclxi "The Lincoln Project," Showtime, Episode 3

cclxii Steinem, Gloria, *My Life on the Road*, Random House, New York, 2015, page 189

cclxiii Parker, Kathleen, *The Washington Post*, July 8, 2020, page A25

cclxiv Cleary, "Sarah Palin and her overarching impact on our political landscape" [cclxv] Brown, "A four-term U.S. senator who went his own way," page A15

[cclxvi] Rosenwald, Michael S., "As FDR sought a fourth term, he knew he was dying," *The Washington Post*, October 8, 2020, page B5

[cclxvii] Scarborough, Joe, "A role model for Joe Biden," *The Washington Post*, November 25, 2020, page A21

[cclxviii] Scarborough, "A role model for Joe Biden," page A21

[cclxix] Holzer, Harold and Garfinkle, Norton, *A Just And Generous Nation,* Basic Books, New York, 2015, page 250

[cclxx] Keegan, John*, The American Civil War,* Knopf, New York, 2009, page 6

[cclxxi] Keegan, *The American Civil War,* page 332

[cclxxii] Keegan, *The American Civil War,* page 64

[cclxxiii] Keegan, *The American Civil War,* page 322

[cclxxiv] Merrill, James M., *William Tecumseh Sherman,* Rand McNally & Company, New York, 1971, page 160

[cclxxv] Keegan, *The American Civil War*, page 65

[cclxxvi] Keegan, *The American Civil War*, pages 172–173

[cclxxvii] Keegan, *The American Civil War,* page 188

[cclxxviii] Alter, Jonathan, *His Very Best: Jimmy Carter, A Life*, Simon and Schuster, New York, 2020, page 228